Pages 28 + 29 - Very good

GOING HER WAY

Books by Father Leo A. Scheetz, M.A., J.C.B.

GOD AND OURSELVES (3 Volumes)

GOD'S RULES FOR THE GAME OF LIFE

GOING HER WAY

MARY, TREE OF LIFE AND OUR HOPE

GOING HER WAY

The Joy of Fifty Years in the Priesthood

Father Leo A. Scheetz, M.A., J.C.B.

An Exposition-Testament Book

Exposition Press   *New York*

IMPRIMATUR

Having been informed by the Reverend William E. Lynch, who has acted as Censor, that the manuscript, *Going Her Way,* has nothing in it contrary to faith and morals and is deserving of a Nihil Obstat, in accordance with the provisions of Canon Law, I grant the necessary Imprimatur to this book. Given at Lafayette this the 19th day of July, 1971.

+ RAYMOND J. GALLAGHER
Bishop of Lafayette-in-Indiana

EXPOSITION PRESS INC.

50 Jericho Turnpike   Jericho, New York 11753

FIRST EDITION

LIBRARY OF CONGRESS CATALOG CARD NUMBER: 70-171715

0-682-47347-2

Foreword

In this most recent book of Father Leo A. Scheetz, the author deals with the subject he knows most intimately, namely, the Priesthood of Jesus Christ. This volume is printed just a few weeks after the celebration of his Golden Anniversary in the Priesthood.

Although the lifetime of service in the Priesthood has given Father Scheetz the opportunity to experience the entire spectrum of joys, sorrows, misunderstandings, criticisms and the like, this volume remains as a strong endorsement of the life and service of a priest to the People of God entrusted to his care.

It should be a very profitable experience for us all to read the words of this book, since it will enable us to see ourselves in one or the other person dealt with in the course of the volume. It should be quite helpful for us to see ourselves as other people do, specifically within the relationships of people, priests, and bishops to the Church. There will be cause for self-examinatoin which all of us will find helpful and salutary.

The joy of being able to spend a lifetime in the Priesthood is the predominant theme of this book. It is an exemplification, in depth, of the constant assertion made by the author. Throughout the Priesthood and notably on the occasion of the 50th Anniversary of Ordination, Father Scheetz has been heard to say that if he had it to do all over again, the Priesthood would still be his choice and his life. We are grateful for the service which Father Scheetz does to the

Priesthood by the manner in which he sets forth in this volume his great devotion. May it be an example for many young men who are still searching for their way of life.

+ RAYMOND J. GALLAGHER
Bishop of Lafayette-in-Indiana

Preface

After fifty years in the priesthood I have been requested to write my autobiography.

Since I am of such little importance by reason of any honors or rights conferred upon me apart from the priesthood, and because I am of considerably less importance in my own right, it is thought best to forego any consideration of my personal life by way of biography. However, if a word from the old and groovy generation might be of some assistance to the newer generation, what with all the present-day dissidence and turmoil, then may the following suffice, or be helpful.

It is not without proper gratitude for every moment of this longevity that I proceed. May what follows serve as a springboard from which to make the leap for the welfare of young clergy, parents, and their children.

The Bible informs us that all paternity is in heaven. Since maternity is an inseparable part of paternity, maternity too must be in heaven. This is to advise that whether married or tempted to get married for the sake of fulfillment, one must never lose sight of the revealed truth that perfect fulfillment in either case can be accomplished only through Him and Her by going Her way, which is His way.

Because of creation the natural must always be both a minus quality and a minus quantity. The addition of the supernatural is required for the completion and the fulfillment of the natural, whether one be married or not. No one was more human than Jesus and Mary. If marriage were required for any further benefit, each of them would have been a full spouse to someone else. The existence of God our Father is co-natural to each one of us because He left the "handprint" of His creation on each one of us. For this reason we knowingly or unknowingly clamor for Him. We cannot get on without Him.

Identification with His Blessed Mother is most useful for the proper fulfillment of anyone's life because He left the handprint for sanctification on everyone: "Woman, behold, thy son." [Son] "Behold, thy mother." For "he that shall find me shall find life and shall have salvation from the Lord."

Might I suggest that it is this "touch" of His and Her "handprint" that is spelling this void in this life of the young priest and the teenager today! It is a yen for the supernatural. But they are trying to sate or to glut this emptiness with the natural or the material to no avail. Did not St. Augustine tell us in his *Confessions* that he wasted the best years of his life, the first thirty-five, over the same thing! He finally awakened to the tragedy of it all when he cried out, "Thou hast made us for thee, O Lord, and our soul is restless until it rests in thee." Augustine admitted to a certain immaturity at the beginning of his best years.

Many of the present-day difficulties might have been prevented long before they had been conceived in the hearts of certain individuals had their parents or tutors only known the great value and power of Her, and of Her intercession in their behalf. Our earthly mother is not enough, nor is the mother of one's children enough, to fill that void, or emptiness.

We ever stand in need of the prowess of our Blessed Mother, who proved Her greatness in matching wits with both the good and the bad angels. Problem children bespeak problem parents if we are humble enough to admit it. Such is the game of life. She procured the success of Her Son's life, Resurrection and Ascension.

If the reader should like to challenge some of the statements in this volume, he might well meet up with a sufficiency in my three volumes, entitled *God and Ourselves,* for the elementary grades as well as for high-schoolers. Also *Mary, Tree of Life and Our Hope* will furnish added food for thought, as will *God's Rules for the Game of Life.**

If this volume appears to be egocentric, that is exactly what it is. It is based on fifty years' experience in the priesthood. It is not written with any view to sing my own praises. It is far too late for any such thing.

I involve myself for the simple reason that I have always felt that true history on most any subject has never been written. This stand or attitude was confirmed years ago when the late Pius XII was nuncio to Berlin previous to his election as the Supreme Pontiff. He attended a banquet in honor of some great historian. Sitting beside the historian at the banquet table in honor of the historian, the Nuncio expressed himself in similar terms, then asked the historian what percentage of history might be considered reliable.

The historian, with a twinkle in his eye, replied, "Perhaps fifty-one per cent."

It is for this reason that I have invoked anecdotes mostly from my own experience which I know to be true. For the same reason I have refrained from quoting alleged stories.

---

*All the above books are obtainable from the publisher, Exposition Press, Inc., 50 Jericho Turnpike, Jericho, N.Y. 11753.

Introduction

At the time of the writing of this manuscript, perhaps the most bruited-about word in the United States is "abortion."

Perhaps some may feel that the author of these lines might better have been aborted some seventy-six years ago.

May 21, 1971, marks my golden jubilee in the priesthood of Jesus Christ. Reminiscing, we are told, is a high sign of senility. Be that as it may, nonetheless the newer generations opt for such reminiscing in order to help close the generation gaps of their historical lives. Friends and acquaintances of various skills and professions love to gather around the jubilarian in order to inquire about the high and low points of such a career during fifty years. It has been suggested that the questions and answers be consigned to writing as a fitting or worthy companion in a practical way to the theory set forth in *God and Ourselves*.

"Jubilee" is a biblical word (*jobal*: horn, in Hebrew). Every fifty or so years the Israelites were wont to usher in a festive season by the tooting of the horn.

In the United States it is customary for our soldiers on Memorial (Decoration) Day and Veterans (Armistice) Day to sound taps, which is a tooting of their own horns in behalf of the dead or even those who were willing to so sacrifice their lives in behalf of their country.

By the same token might one seek umbrage in the tooting of his own horn after serving the Lord's Church for fifty years, especially when he has one foot already in the grave due to a recent stroke, while going Her way.

This book is titled *Going Her Way* because Her way was always His way. Yes, I refer to our Blessed Mother, who is God's masterpiece of creation and sanctification, and one of our own level even if She is not of our own equal nature, and grace's solitary boast.

Her way, of course, is the way of faith, hope, and love founded upon Her sweet humility, and don't let anyone tell you that a stroke does not make one humble. Having a stroke furnishes an occasion for receiving the sacrament of the Holy Anointing, formerly called Extreme Unction, which causes grace that no other sacrament produces.

It gives one an entirely different outlook on the future while it presents many regrets of the past.

Previous to the stroke those who might have twisted my arm in order to get me to put these experiences to writing would have twisted in vain.

Some statements in this volume are not highly commendatory to either Catholics, Protestants, other non-Catholics, Jews, or any other ethnic group. This, because Jesus died with the hope that the whole world would become His and Her followers.

When one is faced with death, one does not pull any punches. Jesus never did. He came to die, and did, to merit grace for His followers.

These stories are not recorded for the purpose of harassing or embarrassing any one, but solely for the sake of cajoling the reader, any reader, every reader, to follow in Her footsteps so as to ensure an everlasting bliss in heaven. No one can afford to take any chances.

This, we ought to know and understand full well, is the sole purpose of our creation. One need not live long upon earth to discover that man does not have here "a lasting city"; and that the Creator had to have something more than despair for us to look forward to. Or else what purpose creation! It was for this purpose that Pope Paul VI pronounced Her Mother of the Church, to be our model.

It is being said on all sides today that there are no absolutes; that truth is not objective; that we can't all see alike. If one has one foot in the grave, that will quickly focus one's sights to see that truth is objective; that there are absolutes; that we all can see alike if we are humble and willing enough to admit it.

It is a mistake, ordinarily, to speak of ten, twenty, thirty, forty, fifty years of experience. For the average person, no matter what his position in life, it should be referred to as one experience, repeated ten, twenty, thirty, forty, fifty times.

Not many priests have had their noses in so many varied phases of life.

What, with a complete layoff the very first year after ordination and being put to bed in a hospital for eight months without a friend, save the little evening-newspaper boy from the nearby Jewish ghetto, there was no one to communicate with. No one ever knocked on the door. Believe it or not, the skin of my mouth began to grow shut on either side, perhaps a quarter of an inch, for lack of communication.

The next three years were spent at the orphans' villa. The ugly truth was discovered there that seems only of late to be coming to light all over the United States.

"Orphans' villa" was a misnomer. In large measure it should have been called a refuge for the children of divorcees. That's what happens when the state takes over the duties of the Church.

The state said years ago: divorce is morally good if you so think or believe. Jesus said "in the beginning it was not so." There are absolutes.

The state by its laws protects legalized adultery and is striving now to legalize and protect murder as it does many other heinous sins and crimes all under the guise of liberty, false liberty which is functional liberty but not moral liberty. This, say the authors of abortion, must be because of "population explosion," whereas the truth of the matter is it is so in order that mankind may overindulge its sexual appetite.

If in the United States we do not back up and do penance as the Blessed Mother asked for at Vladimir in Russia (7th century) and at Fatima (1917) and at Lourdes (about 1854) and many other places, as was done in biblical Ninive, we just may live to rue the day.

Please do not rejoin by crying, "Prophet of doom!" I say we have already too many *profits* of doom. God is not mocked, even if His very immensity cannot be fathomed, so that such are shouting, "God is dead."

Ask the astronauts what they think of God's dimensions. Little wonder that He allows Her, our Blessed Mother, who is perfectly human, but not inhuman, one whose dimensions are somewhat within our grasp because of our own earthly mothers, to be His practical spokeswoman.

The five years following were spent as residential chaplain at a small hospital with a small parish some seven miles removed.

Out of every hundred patients, no more than four could have been Catholics. The remainder were Protestants or non-Catholics. Klu Kluxers, yes; so was everybody else mostly, and his brother or sister.

What a harvest of mental distortions were gleaned during the years both in the hospital and the parish level.

Those five years were followed by another year of schooling at the Catholic University of America in preparation for the post of director of charities for the whole diocese.

This job was of brief duration. It lasted long enough to learn what the big cities in America are only learning and living with today.

As a troubleshooter for the bishop I was sent to another parish. There the bishop buried me; he forgot where I was.

This, after a letter to him answering his question, which letter he misinterpreted. He had written and asked if I liked the new assignment. I had always heard that one should be diplomatic. Since I was delighted to get out of the charity office, which to me seemed to be largely a game of protection for the social ills of mankind, I wrote simply without any trimmings to be misinterpreted or condemnatory, "I'm content to be able to spit on my own stove after almost ten years in the priesthood as a chaplain." There was no mention made of whether I liked it or not.

This parish work lasted seventeen and a half years, when I was whisked to another parish across the state for twelve years following the death of the pastor.

The remainder of the fifty years, namely ten years, have been lived out at my present address.

Who I am and what I am has always been a distinction with a tremendous difference and no misgivings on my part.

This distinction was best set forth over forty years ago by a woman who allegedly said, "As a man I do not like Father. But as a priest he can't be beat."

That was the best compliment I ever had for the simple reason it spelled out the philosophy of my own life or living thoughts.

Most people always put their best foot forward first, allowing all connections thereafter to make their own discoveries to the contrary.

My lot was just the opposite. If people received me with my worst foot forward, then I felt they were receiving not the man but the priest, which opted for a good finish.

I am not advocating this philosophy for the shopkeeper or the businessman. But I do advocate it for the priest. Why be a hail-fellow-well-met? Then when someone wants or needs a priest, he will never think of the hail-fellow: he will want a priest.

Since our Lord selected St. Paul to be his missionary, it

appeared that Paul was worth imitating. Some of his words remain as masterful matters to be followed:

"But I will gladly spend and be spent myself for your souls, even though loving you more I be loved less" (II Cor. 12:15).

"Am I now seeking the favor of men, or of God? Or am I seeking to please men? If I were still trying to please men, I should not be a servant of Christ." (Gal. 1:10.)

About the time of my ordination I chanced upon a news item. It referred to the celebration of some successful priest ninety years old out in Oregon. At the banquet the M.C. asked him if he could impart a bit of advice to the youngsters there present. The old priest said, "As I think about it one should have a few complexes that ever drive him on and on, both on the material and the supernatural level.

"First of all there is the death of our Lord which should drive us on and on.

"Secondly, there is the Blessed Virgin Mother and Her way, with Her power of intercession demonstrated at the wedding feast of Cana. Her authority over Her Son, who is God. She gave Him just a little nudge, only a hint: 'They have no wine.' He took care of it right then."

Continuing, the old priest said, "There should be one or two things on the national level that get under one's skin and drive him on and on the rest of his life. Perhaps we could call it 'one's pet peeves.' "

What that old priest mentioned on the supernatural level I already was saturated with because of my good papa and mamma. But the pet peeves were not long in forthcoming. Divine Providence's timing is always most appropriate if we have sense enough to recognize it.

About the time referred to above I was returning on the train from the seminary in Cincinnati to my home in Lafayette. I occupied a double seat, alone with my thoughts. Pretty soon a gentleman with a nose large enough to shake hands with stopped and asked, "Do you mind if I sit next to you?" Immediately the conversation brought this question from my newly found friend: "How many Catholics in the U.S.A.?" I answered, "twenty million." (Today there are some 40 million, just double in 54 years.) My friend quietly replied: "Oh, my goodness. We Jews are only six million. If we had that many we'd run the country. We almost run it now," he said.

That statement, of course, has stuck in my subconscious mind all these years. Here we are, every man, woman and child sent as missionaries by the Lord to bear witness to His truths. Our influence is practically nil. As Paul says, all authority is from God (Romans). We allow the state to usurp His authority under the guise of false liberty and to use it to defend sin and crime.

It is quite proper for the state to show compassion to the sinner, but never to put a premium and protection upon crime with its laws.

During the Christmas vacation that brought me home that year I boarded a streetcar near the depot. I was scarcely seated, when an elderly Protestant lady turned around and asked me to come to her Sunday-school class. She was doing missionary work. I loved her for it.

At home a Protestant minister stopped me on the street. He asked me to come and become a Christian: a member of his church.

Where were the Catholics, despite the fact they had received the robur (strength) of Confirmation? They were cowards, afraid to be missionaries for Christ.

On the return trip to the seminary a gentleman and I occupied the same seat in a crowded train. Our conversation brought out this revealing fact that still motivates me as much as anything yet. It might be called a complex. He said, "You know I am a Catholic Christian and an actor on the theatrical stage, mostly on Broadway.

"I hate to say this, but it is true: I have listened to many sermons over the years of my life. Seldom have I ever heard what I would call a good one. It has always seemed to me that the priest in the pulpit halfway apologizes for what he is saying lest he hurt someone's feelings. In other words, most priests preach the truth as if it were fiction, whereas we actors speak fiction as if it were the truth."

The foregoing paragraphs furnish the ideas that have largely formed the pattern for my priestly life and will still be recognized today in this very volume.

This pattern of behavior caused me to make a deal with the Blessed Mother and the forgotten person of the Holy Trinity, the Holy Spirit, who since Gabriel's "hour" have been spouses to each other. I promised them if they would inspire me what to say when in the pulpit or in private, I would say it and take the heat. So thus have I had the heat for fifty years. Years later Harry S said it well: "If you can't take the heat, then get out of the kitchen."

Yes, I was always in the "kitchen."

Yes, I was always familiar with Francis de Sales' slogan: "You can catch more flies with honey than with vinegar." But I was also deeply cognizant of what our Lord said to me at ordination, "I send you forth to catch men: to be fishers of men." He never said a word about catching flies.

Too many have been catching flies this long time, so today they do not know what to do with all the flies that are swarming about.

Most people think our Lord was a candy kid or a sort of cream puff, according to their own making or liking. He was not. If you read His life in the New Testament, you will discover He was anything but. He attacked the Establishment of that day. He called names and put everyone in his proper place. Neither did He curry favor, or any sycophancy.

There was another principle that guided my priestly actions. Whereas most people pray, "God help me to do *my* work," I've always prayed: "God, help me to do Your work. You started this religion. It's yours, not mine, so if I put bark to my words, it is because of you." An ounce of prevention is worth a ton of cure.

There is quite a distinction between putting bark to one's words beforehand in order to prevent anything untoward, and putting mildness in one's actions after a mistake, in order to show clemency or compassion.

This makes us think of what one of my councilmen said to me forty years ago: "Father, the trouble with you is that when you want something you want it right now." So I said to him, "I'm like the fellow who lived alone. His long-lost buddy called on him to pay a visit. In looking around, the visitor noticed three holes at the bottom of an outside door. So he asked what for. He got this reply: 'I have three cats and three holes for the cats to go out of.' 'Wouldn't one hole be enough?' he was asked. He replied, 'Man, you know, when I say scat, I mean scat."

Anent the point of catching flies with honey, etc., I always preferred the saying you catch bees with honey or they'll sting you. In this case the bees are the children. The kiddies for fifty years have always been my solace. I was never stung by them.

My life has never been in polishing the apple. Rather it has been spent in striving to get God's people to love Him and Our Lady. He must increase and I must decrease, as St. Paul said. And there has been considerable success, as all agree wherever I've been.

My batting average for the first forty years was thirteen converts a year. The national figures were less than two per priest.

As the Protestants say: "We must bring God to the people, not wait until the people come to God."

Due credit for the above is due to God and going Her way, not to me.

PART ONE

1

It is to be hoped that the reader will see in the word "joy" used in the following section the word borrowed from the Bible which is of supernatural vintage: "Let us . . . run with patience to the fight set before us; looking towards . . . Jesus, who for . . . *joy* . . . endured a cross" (Heb. 12:1-2).

The word "joy" will always be used in the singular when it equates with God, who is One; and is on the supernatural level. The other word "joy" of the natural sphere may be pluralized—but only on the natural level. Surely our dear Lord endured no natural joys during His Passion. Nonetheless, St. Paul says He endured the cross "for *joy*." His own blessed Mother must have afforded Him many natural joys during life.

These lines are written in the wake of the recent copious despicable tears shed by dissidents of discontent, dissatisfaction, disillusionment, despair, distraction, destruction, discouragement, disorientation, derangement, and desertion concerning our dear Lord's priesthood.

Their tears have been flooding the market called the news media in multifarious forms. It has gotten to be big business both for the media, which have been exploiting it for all it is worth, and for the exploited.

It is high time someone came to the rescue or defense of our dear Lord and His priesthood—being witness thereto, as they say today. These lines purport to do just that, because a slap at the priesthood is a slap at our dear Lord, and a slap at our dear Lord is a slap at one's self. He put joy in the priesthood if we know how to find it.

This is not to say that this article is to be a broadside against those who have defected. Far from that. But it is to say it is meant to be an attack on Satan. I hate him: he has been after me all of my fifty years in the priesthood. He gained many victories over me for which I am still sorry. Yet my faith still engenders hope that love will be my lot in the end, and that joy in the priesthood shall never pass away.

There is nothing wrong with the priesthood, albeit there may be, and is, plenty that is wrong with the priests who compose His priesthood—with this writer included in generous measure.

Jesus knew how imperfect we are when He called us, just as He did when He called the first priests, the Twelve: "If, therefore, I the Lord and Master have washed your feet, you also ought to wash the feet of one another" (John 13:14).

What is more, that same Jesus who elected Simon to be Peter the first Pope and His Vicar foreknew that even he would sin. Despite that foreknowledge Jesus promised Peter the office, and later on put him in it, as the "Pappa," the head of His Church, to which He attached infallibility in matters of divine religion.

While Jesus gave assurance—not that Peter *would* not err in matters of "Faith and morals," but that he *could* not err, and therefore would not err, Jesus never gave Peter any assurance that he would not or could not sin. Peccability is a human personal matter. It comes with the person and belongs to the person as a part of his freedom, so that he may gain merit and merit heaven. But infallibility is an official matter. It comes with and belongs to the office of Vicar of Christ (Matt. 16:18).

Even though Jesus had already promised Peter the office of Vicar, together with its infallibility, nonetheless Jesus did call the turn on Peter by telling him he was due for a fall. Infallibility would be in Jesus' hands; therefore is the Pope

His Vicar. But the life of the man would be in his own hands, and therefore is he a sinner: "Simon, Simon," He said, "behold, Satan has desired to have you, that he may sift you as wheat. But I have prayed for you, that your faith may not fail; and do you, once you are converted, confirm your brethren" (Luke 22:31-32).

Here it is interesting to note, as confirming the point made above, that when Jesus promised the papacy, He called him "Peter" (Matt. 16:18). But when He promised that the roosters would be crowing in his ears early some morning, Jesus used his family name, "Simon, Simon."

A further observation is in order: Jesus prayed that Simon's faith would not fail. And Simon's faith did not fail, because of that prayer. But His morals failed him. Simon did not deny his faith that Jesus is God. He simply swore, "I know not the man" (Luke 22:60,72).

Be it said here out of deference to all priests, Simon was not the only man to hear roosters crowing in the early morning, and what is more, he was not destined to be the last one. Jesus knows that too, but still He calls us to the priesthood.

That particular experience of Simon's, and perhaps other unrecorded experiences, he capitalized on when later, as acting Pope, he wrote his first encyclical:

> Now I exhort the presbyters among you—I, your fellow-presbyter and witness of the sufferings of Christ, the partaker also of the glory that is to be revealed in time to come—tend the flock of God which is among you, governing not under constraint, but willingly, according to God; nor yet for the sake of base gain, but eagerly; nor yet as lording it over your charges, but becoming from the heart a pattern to the flock. And when the Prince of the shepherds appears, you will receive the unfading crown of glory. Likewise, you who are younger, be sub-

ject to the presbyters. And all of you practise humility towards one another; for, "God resists the proud, but gives grace to the humble." Humble yourselves, therefore, under the mighty hand of God, that he may exalt you in the time of visitation, cast all your anxiety upon him, because he cares for you. Be sober, be watchful! For your adversary the devil, as a roaring lion, goes about seeking someone to devour. Resist him steadfast in the faith, knowing that the same suffering befalls your brethren all over the world. But the God of all grace, who has called us unto his eternal glory in Christ Jesus, will himself, after we have suffered a little while, perfect, strengthen and establish us. [I Pet. 5:1-10]

Surely these words of Peter, the Pope, inspired as they must be, though not infused knowledge, in part describe and circumscribe the goings on of Simon, the man, the night the roosters crowed so very, very audibly; the night Simon the man, out of curiosity, and loyalty too, no doubt, got himself confronted with the sharp tongues of women—and were they barmaids!; the night Simon, the man, in his pride belied his own previous boast: "Lord, with thee I am ready to go both to prison and to death!" (Luke 22:33).

The alleged reasons, or would it be truer to say the unalleged reasons, advanced today for defecting from the priesthood might well have been prevented had Pope Peter's advice been heeded. Surely Simon's experience would not have taken place had he heeded a wiser head, that of His Lord and Master.

Pope Peter advises the younger ministers to be subject to the elders. That of course calls for humility, as Peter indicated: "Be humbled under the mighty hand of God." And God does have a way of humbling us, as Simon found out, for not avoiding the proximate occasion of sin; and for not praying. Surely one's own sins, not the sins of the pastor or even of the bishop, are the ample reason for humility. And truthfully, which is it, one's own sins or the sins of the pastor, that give rise to the most "anxiety" of which Peter writes? In any event Pope Peter says, "Cast your cares on Jesus, for he has care of you."

It is interesting how Pope Peter likens Satan's assaults to a "roaring lion." Undoubtedly that night the roosters crowed, Simon's head was roaring, swelled as it was with pride on that fateful night—the night the women gave him a bad time; the night they razzed him because of his Galilean accent betraying him.

Simon also learned then, if he had never learned it before during his own marriage, that God has not yet made a man who can outsmart a woman.

Simon was never to forget the experience. Would that we might profit the more from our experiences. The defectors today and tomorrow should learn from Simon: if they don't always keep the morals, at least they should know their dogma. Had they known their dogma, they would have said, "I'd rather fight than switch. I'd rather remain in the priesthood than out of it." That is, play it cool.

Speaking from experience, I would say every one of the defectors must have been a man of great talent. If they were nobodies, Satan would not have wasted his time on them. But then, no priest is a nobody, or he never would have become a priest. This isn't pride. It is humility if one gives the credit to God and to the Church who makes every priest a somebody worth while. These defectors, despite periodic falls, might have stayed on to become great saints. It is not too late yet. Why allow Satan a complete victory! Satan, that old prevaricator, promises everything, but in reality he has not a thing to offer of permanency, save hell.

Little wonder Pope Peter cautions, "Be sober, be watchful." He might have gone on to say, "what happened to me can easily happen to you. And oh, boy, how it hurts—the rest of one's life."

Paul understood the weaknesses in human nature. He had a fine word of encouragement for the downhearted priest. He said the priest called as Aaron was will offer the sacrifice of the altar (worthily of course, and not sacrilegiously), first for his own sins and then for the sins of the people: "For every high priest taken from among men is appointed for men in the things pertaining to God, that he may offer gifts and sacrifices for sins. He is able to have compassion on the ignorant and erring, because he himself also is beset with weakness, and by reason thereof is obliged to offer for sins, as on behalf of the people, so also for himself." (Heb. 5:1-4.)

If pride will not keep one from committing sin, then pride should not keep one from confessing them. That's what faith teaches. This is not to write in defense of sin. But it is to come to the defense of repentant sinners, and to bespeak the mercy and clemency of God.

Jesus knew and foretold that Satan, who had the arrogance to tempt Him, would surely not spare His priests. He says, "The world [of Satan] will hate you. And you will be hated [by Satan] for my name's sake—because of me, that is.

Then, by way of implication, just to let it be known that not everyone de facto will always be, at all times, equal to the fight, Jesus followed up by saying, "But he who perseveres to the end shall be saved" (Matt. 10:22). What else is perseverance for the average person if not a periodic series of lapses, of falls with repeated resurrections!

Was St. Augustine thinking on the Master's words about "perseverance" when he said that grace runs as in a chain. But the grace of final perseverance is a special grace all of its own!

One may lose many or all of the battles with Satan, but

if he wins the last one, he will be persevering to the end, and he will be saved.)

It takes courage, fortitude, to withstand the assaults of Satan. But that fortitude, that courage, that *robur,* is an infused virtue that has been given to every priest. And perseverance is born of that robur. What the priest needs to do is not to be afraid to use that robur.

The remark is heard all too frequently from thoughtless priests, yes, priests who are confessors, but outside the "box," of course, concerning certain of their confreres: "They ought to defect rather than live the way they do." Such nonsense! As if defecting were not living in sin. Such would be living their lives sealed in sin. Why not hold out a helping hand rather than wish their confreres such evil! Why not hold up the words Paul wrote to his priests: "Let us run with patience to the fight set before us, looking towards . . . Jesus, who for joy . . . endured the cross" (Heb. 12:2). Joy is permanent. Sinful pleasure, and there are many kinds, is a fleeting thing. The only permanent thing about sinful pleasure is the hold Satan gets on one if one does not "watch and pray"; or with that certain kind of devil of which Jesus said, "That kind can be cast out only by prayer and fasting" (Matt. 17:20).

The gentle St. John, whom we believe to be a virgin, was most understanding and compassionate. Consider what he wrote with such delicate finesse after having lived almost a hundred years:

> My dear children, these things I write to you in order that you may not sin. But if anyone sins, we have an advocate with the Father, Jesus Christ the just; and he is a propitiation for our sins, not for ours only but for those of the whole world. (I John 2:1-2.)

These lines are being written by one who has spent fifty

years in the priesthood, not with any intent of fostering a presumption of God's mercy, but rather to accentuate His mercy; to dissipate the fog of despair or discouragement; to prevent those who know not "the depths of Satan" (Apoc. 2:24) from crying, "I'm lonesome" upon the shoulders of certain tools of Satan, always waiting in readiness to oblige with their satanical promise of fulfillment which brings with it not only defection but especially morbid lonesomeness.

There is no use in being more nor less Catholic than the Scriptures. Nor is there any place here for either rigorism or laxity. But there is a place, and now is the time, for compassion of Jesus, who "cares for you." This time let us appeal again to Simon's precocity: "Then Peter came up to him and said, "Lord how often shall my brother sin against me, and I forgive him? Up to seven times? Jesus said to him, 'I do not say to thee seven times, but seventy times seven.'" (Matt. 18:21-22.)

Compassion, pity, mercy, are the words ever in the heart of the eternal High Priest, and upon His lips. After all, who died for sins: the confessor, or He whose place the confessor fills! The way some confessors act before, during, and after a confession, one would think it was they who died for sins. Some even close human relations thereafter to the one they have just shriven; and this is not hearsay.

Here the words of the old pro St. Augustine come to mind: "Whenever I hear [he didn't say where he heard it—in the box or out of it] of some one having done wrong; I cannot condemn him. For I know if I had been in the same circumstances, I would have done far worse than that one."

Our Lord equated joy and happiness with suffering. The priest is destined for suffering as well as joy in this life. The Beatitudes all begin with the same word, "Happy," even the one that refers to persecution and insult provided it be done and accepted for His name's sake. True love likes to suffer. Suffering for Him is love's joy.

The whole life of Christ, and therefore that of His true priests, is wrapped up in the enigmatic paradox of mystery that identifies joy with suffering and suffering with joy. And please, Mr. Psychologist, do not call it masochistic complex, or schizophrenia, or paranoia. Paul was not a "schizo," yet he was able to exclaim, "I overflow with *joy* in all your troubles" (II Cor. 7:9). Paul knew how to identify with joy and suffering at the same time: the one is of the supernatural, the other of the natural, vintage.

Joy is a built-in phenomenon of suffering endured for the Lord. For the one, finally experienced—and it seems to take a long time—joy is antecedent to, accompanies, follows and surrounds suffering. It is much like understanding and faith. For "if you do not believe, you will not understand" (Isa. 7:9).

Augustine finally caught onto this from experience, so he said, "Credo ut intelligam"—"I believe in order to understand." So every priest must catch onto the enigma of suffering in the priesthood in order to prosper the joy of his priestly life. Jesus told us this: "You shall weep and lament, but the world [of Satan] shall rejoice; and you shall be sorrowful, but your *joy* no one [man or woman] shall take from you" (John 16:20-22). If man or woman cannot take it from you, they cannot confer it either. It must come from Him and Her.

Faith teaches us that it is a joy in itself to be a priest realizing that the priesthood is an indispensable instrument for the salvation and redemption of mankind. When the priest desires that end for God and for mankind, then surely suffering, frustration, loneliness, and irrelevance, which are indispensable means to that indispensable end, will have to be a joy, a great, great joy.

Our Lady knew all of this already at the age of fifteen when She sang Her Magnificat in sweet humility: "My soul magnifies the Lord, and my spirit *rejoices* in God my Savior." What else is this but Her profession of faith that identifies suffering in His name with joy; and joy with suffering! She is the Mother of fair love. She is the Mother of joy while at the same time She is the Mother of Sorrows.

Can we priests, Her precious sons, ever hope to be otherwise than was our Blessed Mother! Why do some give up Holy Orders in order to take on unholy orders from some earthly woman. Why not go *Her* way!

Joy and sorrow, therefore, are in the priesthood by divine design, after original sin. It is the priestly vocation. It is to be found in the very exercise of the priestly ministry. This ministry is not a gift for the priest—but to the priest to be expended generously for others: to carry on the Work of redemption and salvation.

It matters not what seeming frustrations might be forthcoming because of the bishop, a pastor, or some confrere; such suffering cannot take away that joy which is identified with our priesthood. This, to repeat, for the simple reason that spiritual joy, not joys, and suffering are inseparable from, and indispensable to, each other.

Faith teaches that the priesthood is a divine joy. Experience teaches that it is fraught with suffering that is very human. To repeat, faith teaches both suffering and joy are of the very essence of the priesthood, because that is what Jesus taught and lived. His Blessed Mother lived it.

May, therefore, Jesus be always in our heart when the going is tough, and may Mary be always at our side, as Jesus will say in each Mass: "Woman, behold, thy son! [Son], Behold, thy mother!" (John 19:26-27).

Such is the joy, such is the suffering, we bargained for when we accepted the call to His priesthood.

2

Words, the same as money, can be counterfeit. In the realm of religion this is only too true. Witness the motley of meanings in Christianity today.

If words were money, people would not be long in ascertaining their genuineness. Since they are not, truth and error can go on without too much concern. Such is the disinterest in religion.

To test them, words must be dropped on the anvil of truth to hear the sound of their ring. In the field of His religion our Lord affords us the anvil. The anvil upon which He hammers out the verbal mintage of His revealed truth in man's words is the Bible, under His Vicar's guidance, whenever and however he speaks.

This fact should immediately alert one to the supernatural order. Unfortunately, not too many people arise above the natural order in their thinking. That was Judas' trouble (John 6:65). And that is one of the troubles with today's so-called demythologizing of the Scriptures. This prevents a proper relating with the supernatural order, and prevents the word of God from coming alive in the priest so that he may relate to God person to person.

When this supernatural relating ceases, the priest will find himself sweltering in discontent, dissatisfaction, despair, and frustration a-griping about what is wrong with the priesthood. It scarce occurs to him that there is nothing wrong with the priesthood, but that there may be plenty that is wrong with him both as a man and as a priest.

On the natural level, the words joy and pleasure may be synonymous. Such is not true on the supernatural level, where the relevance is one of personal contact with Christ.

Joy in the priesthood is a spiritual joy, a supernatural joy, a heavenly joy. Jesus promises the very opposite of pleasure, or earthly joy, in the joy He puts in His priesthood. Indeed, He promises suffering as a harbinger of His joy.

Golf and bridge and athletics are not a part of the priesthood per se. However, they may be and are necessary elements for the man who is a priest. To some they are earthly joys. To others they may not be. But in either case the result is the same whether one be a priest or not.

The joy in the priesthood is divine. It is heavenly: "A body thou hast fitted me. Behold, I come to do thy will." The words "Thou art my beloved Son, in whom I am well pleased" were spoken by the Father, not because of Jesus' hobbies, such as making yoke and boats—not crosses, as the artists are so fond of depicting Him—but because He was to be the priest and victim.

Jesus said to His priests: "Behold, I am sending you forth like sheep in the midst of wolves. . . . And you will be hated by all for my name's sake . . . and [persecuted]. . . . Do not think I have come to send peace upon the earth; I have come to bring a sword, not peace." (Matt. 10:16 ff.).

Surely there is not much comfort in such an outlook to one who is looking for earthly joy and pleasure. The plane upon which Jesus operates in His priesthood, with its joy, supersedes even human love: even the love of consanguinity and affinity: "He who loves father or mother . . . son or daughter more than me is not worthy of me. And he who does not take up his cross and follow me, is not worthy of me . . . and a man's enemies will be those of his own household." (*Ibid.*)

The joy of the priesthood has to be discovered by trial and error with perseverance. The thing that has to be learned from experience is all that Jesus included in that one terse word: "Take up your cross daily" (Luke 9:23). To believe what Jesus said is one thing, and to personalize that faith is quite another—even when one is willing. This takes faith and the Holy Spirit. It takes a lot of doing, as we shall see later on.

Shortly after my ordination an older priest quoted a still older priest, of some certain fame, as having said: "The day will come when you would wish to tear from you that collar by which Rome has you by the neck." Of course, I was shocked at such words. As I grew older I learned there were many who were in such throes. Then the words of Paul came to my mind: No one is lawfully crowned unless he will first have been tried. This holds true for any vocation or avocation in life and as such should not be too disturbing. Joy is certified by suffering.

Satan has always tempted and tried to lure men away from Christ. Satan tempts to evil. Christ tempts to good. It is that simple. And upon the outcome there results merit or demerit because of free will.

If there is anyone whom Satan desires to have a fall, it must be the priest. Such being the case, if the priest is alert, there can be no greater priestly joy than "to put on the armor of faith and repel the fiery darts of the most wicked one" (Eph. 6:16). Only in this way will he derive the greatest fulfillment in his priesthood. The fight is on from the very day of ordination, one way or another, whether in preaching the Word, or the Good News, or in distributing goods to the poor. In any event Satan will find some ruse to create suffering. The drives of our nature are at cross purposes oftentimes with the urges of grace and thereby is formed the "cross we must take up daily."

Often one's own personality presents conflicts which must be suffered. St. Francis of Assisi, we read, used to pray, as did Cardinal Merry del Val, "to be misunderstood." I never had to do that.

If we wish to live by the Spirit of Christ—and every priest should—we will have to "walk with that Spirit." In doing this

He will give up His fruit: "charity, joy, peace, patience, kindness, goodness, faith, modesty, continency" (Gal. 5:22-25), the assets for joy in the priesthood.

Pope Peter must have experienced much about the deception from self-fulfillment as we do today. He wrote, "All flesh is as grass and all its glory as the flower of grass; the grass withered, and the flower has fallen" (I Pet. 1:24).

Jesus too had fulfillment in mind. He knew there was such a thing as natural human love. Yet He laid His stress upon divine love solely, for those who could take it (Matt. 19:12) for His priesthood. He said, "Abide in my love. If you keep my commandments you will abide in his love. These things I have spoken to you that my joy may be in you, and that your joy may be made full" (John 15:9 ff.). Some will object and say that everyone must keep His commandments. This is true, but the words just quoted from the Lord were addressed by Him to His first priests. They had special commandments to keep: preaching, offering the sacrifice, practicing celibacy, and the other works of the ministry.

The joy of His priesthood, therefore, is the reward which Jesus attaches here and now for the painful fulfilling of all the priest's responsibilities of his ministry: "Amen, amen, I say to you, that you shall weep and lament, but the world [of Satan] shall rejoice; and you shall be sorrowful, but your sorrow shall be turned into joy. . . . and your joy no one shall take from you," not even in this life (John 16:20,22, 24).

Today the materialistic psychologists would scoff at such words from our Lord. They will say they are bound to lead to some form of insanity. One unfortunate thing about the psychologists is that the most that they know is the residue of their studies of abnormal people. Jesus knew what He was talking about. He was a victim priest, and He asks His priests to come after Him to be victim priests. Yet Jesus was never of unsound mind, although the Pharisees and His enemies thought He was: "He has a devil and is mad" (John 10:20).

The one thing to remember is this: Jesus, the divine psychologist, furnishes His special grace of the supernatural order, which grace has or produces its own euphoria (well-being). Jesus puts it this way: "Hitherto you have not asked anything in My name. Ask and you shall receive, that your joy may be full" (John 16:24).

In the beginning those who were to become His priests, "the twelve," were weary clods (I speak not disrespectfully). They needed to be educated. And Jesus did educate them, and assist them with His grace; and after they were filled with the Holy Ghost, they "took off" and all were heard from "save the son of perdition."

Jesus never trained them to try to go it alone, without Him, and expect to get their job done. Their life, which involved their whole personality, (more than one's stomach) called for living by the code, His code. He never gracefully smothered a sinister code of living that could be continued along with His requirements. In other words, He never said, "When you eat too well, take Di-Gel." No; He said, "Keep my commandments and pray; pray and keep my commandments, and all will be joy even if there is suffering which is sure to come because of Satan."

Jesus was always down to earth with His explanation of heavenly doctrine. He found an apt comparison in a woman about to give birth, as a suitable example of portraying the many spiritual parturitions His future priests would have to undergo if they were to have true fulfillment in their life as priests. He said: "A woman about to give birth has sorrow, because her hour has come. But when she has brought forth the child, she no longer remembers the anguish for her *joy* that a man is born into the world. And you therefore have sorrow now; but I will see you again, and your heart shall rejoice, and your joy no one shall take from you." (John 16:21-22.)

While Jesus compared the heavenly joy of His priests in their priestly work to the earthly joy of a woman in childbirth, in their many labors, He pressed the comparison no further. That is to say, Jesus did not state how long the priest's labor pains would last, nor how frequently the pains of labor would recur. The point He was making was that every priest would have to pay a certain price of suffering for the joy of his priesthood; and that the joy would be worth the price.

Here I would like to draw a further point from the woman and her child experience. One time a priest happened to be on the floor of the O.B. ward in a certain hospital. The sister nurse on the floor said to the priest "There is one thing that has been bothering me for a long time. When these mothers are having their labor pains and are carrying on to the effect, 'Believe me, I'll never have another child,' should I scold them and tell them that is wrong to say that, or to talk that way." The priest said, "Sister, you are not very understanding. Just smile when they talk like that. In another year or so they will be back again to occupy your ward." The joy in having a baby is worth all the anguish.

Such might be the comparison for the priest at times. He might find himself in a nasty type of suffering to such an extent that he promises himself he will never again be so caught. It might be the criticism that comes from his sermons. The suffering is almost too much to take. But when he sits in the box and discovers that someone has come to unload because of his very sermon for which he got a bad time, maybe even from his bishop, the old urge of divine grace, when it comes, will inspire him to carry on, because of the joy that a sinner was reborn to God. Bishops, too, often prefer appeasement and what they call peace, which really is not peace at all. It is only a sense of quiet that prevails in a parish where the people are left on their own and are not disturbed. There are so many people who think they are religious, yet at the same time never let our Lord's religion interfere with their lives.

Satan always knows when a priest will be doing good with his sermons, and he is on the job to bestir certain people who know they have the bishop's ear. Why not remember the Church knows Satan is up to his old tricks even during the sermons? That is why the Church has holy water at the entrance when the old boy comes riding in on a person's shoulder. Any priest who does a good job in the pulpit will meet with caustic suffering. And all because of Satan, as a rule.

For years now we have been hearing that you can catch more flies with honey than with vinegar. Well, we are having the flies now. They are truly swarming, if flies swarm. Our Lord said, "Henceforth you shall catch men" (Luke 5:10). He too was in ill repute because of His sermons, and what a joy it was for Him to go to Calvary after having been misunderstood by the clergy of the synagogue. His enemies even had Him connected with the "god of flies."

It has often been said that the underworld is running our country, referring to the pressure the underworld is able to bring to bear on public officials. And in part that is true, though it would be difficult to prove. The same thing has been bruited about for many years in the Church. One hates to think so; and scarce anyone would admit it, but all the same, how about the many priests who have quit preaching sermons, sermons of value, just because they have been cautioned to "tone down." The pastors around the country will tell you the missionaries no longer have their touch; good people will tell you the same thing. This all adds up to the sufferings Jesus was talking about if one does one's duty in a conscientious way. In the seminary we were taught the injunctions in the Bible: "You must be fools for Christ's sake." But the active ministry came up with a new touch to that one and harangued, "For Christ's sake, don't be a fool."

The joy Jesus spoke about is the joy one is to experience in this life, which of course will lead to the joy of life eternal. It is a joy which "no eye has seen nor ear heard, nor has it entered into the heart of man, what things God has prepared for those who love him" (I Cor. 2:9).

This joy is to be experienced here and now, and is not, as so many writers erroneously state, a joy reserved only for the hereafter. Eternal life and heavenly joy begin now if we qualify for it. It comes from the Holy Spirit of Christ. When Jesus said to His priests, the Twelve, who were disconsolate, "I will see you again," He was referring to His return with the Father through the Holy Spirit, the spirit of joy.

In writing the Acts, Luke tells of one of Paul's masterful deliveries in bearing witness to the Good News (Acts 13:1ff.).

In the face of opposition "many of the Jews and the worshipping converts went away with Paul and Barnabas, and they talked with them and urged them to hold fast to the grace of God. And . . . almost the whole city gathered to hear the word of the Lord. But on seeing the crowds, the Jews were filled with jealousy and contradicted what was said by Paul, and blasphemed. . . . the Jews . . . stirred up a persecution against Paul and Barnabas and drove them from their district. But they shook off the dust of their feet [Matt. 10:14] in protest against them. . . . And the disciples continued to be filled with joy and with the Holy Spirit" (Acts 13:43, 50-52). While the preaching was accompanied with persecution, pain, and suffering, nonetheless "they continued to be filled with joy and with the Holy Spirit."

This "fill of joy and the Holy Spirit" was what Jesus was promising in His homily at the first Mass after the Last Supper, when addressing Himself to His Heavenly Father, He referred to His own leaving and the coming of the Holy Spirit, in the following words: "Father . . . now I am coming to thee; and these things I speak in the world, in order that they may have my joy made full in themselves. I have given them thy word; and the world [of Satan] has hated them, because they are not of the world [of Satan], even as I am not of the world [of Satan]." (John 17:12-17.)

Little wonder that Paul wrote to the Romans, "The kingdom of God [consists in] justice and peace and joy in the Holy Spirit" (Rom. 14:17).

The words spoken to His priests already quoted above from Jesus are to be believed by His priests: not with a mere assent of the mind and will, but with the whole personality of doing. Words believed, which contain a promise, must necessarily engender a true hope. The promise is clear. It is joy promised to His priests who perform the Lord's commands to His priests. The promise, therefore, carries with it the hope of joy. It is the promise that made Paul write, "Now may the God of Hope fill you with all joy and peace in believing, that you may abound in hope and in the power of the Holy Spirit" (Rom. 15:13).

Priests, therefore, who lose sight of the teachings of faith concerning the joy to be found in their priesthood as unveiled, or hammered out on the anvil of the Sacred Scriptures are sooner or later bound to become disoriented, disheartened, disenchanted, unfulfilled malcontents of frustration.

Such are ripe for an exposé of their "innards" on TV, that mighty weapon of propaganda which Satan was quick to grab for the purpose of violence to Christ and to His Church. May we pray for their return! May we at the same time pray for our own perseverance and that of all priests that our joy may be full in the midst of suffering!

3

In my own early years in the priesthood, had the times been the same as they are today for young priests, it is difficult to say what might have become of me. However, there is no reason to speculate upon idle hypotheses. Suffice it to tell what actually happened.

Perhaps I too was a mother's spoiled brat—as are most boys who go on for the priesthood—as someone so aptly described the average priest's early background. But be that as it may, somehow a taste for the Holy Scriptures, developed in the seminary, brought me in constant meditation on the teachings of our Lord to His first priests. That teaching was exemplified in the Passion of our Lord and in His life. His word and example afforded that "hope of joy" which He promised to His priests, while at the same time promising them suffering even unto martyrdom.

The first years were the most difficult. It takes time to develop that divine sense of humor which sees, lurking behind the doings of men (even men of the cloth), the machinations of the "Prince of this world's darkness" (Eph. 6:12); and to comprehend "the depths of Satan" (Apoc. 2:24).

It takes time to wrestle with the mystery of suffering contained in the divine paradox that identifies joy with suffering. It takes time to figure out how "a man's enemies shall be those of his own household" (Matt. 10:36)—the "household of faith" (Gal. 6:10), that is. It takes time to recover from the sudden shock thereof. It takes time, plus God's grace, which one must remember to pray for, to enable one to say with the old pro St. Paul, "I overflow with joy in all *our* troubles" (II Cor. 7:4). It also takes time, plus God's grace, to be in that enviable position where one will have the courage to say and to do, with Paul, "We, however, are not those who draw back unto destruction, but of those who have faith to the saving of the soul" (Heb. 10:39).

The key to the divine sense of humor is afforded also by Paul. Once his words are fixed firmly in one's life there is not too much difficulty in saying to oneself, "I count it a joy to suffer for the cause of Christ. For power is made firm in suffering."

No matter what work of the Lord a priest undertakes, sooner or later, mostly sooner, every priest worth his salt will of necessity meet with opposition, persecution, and suffering. If this persecution does not arise from the nature of the work, then it will come either because of personality or from the devil, or both. This, every priest must be prepared to look for, and know how to meet, or he will soon become discouraged. In his discouragement he just might find himself crying on the wrong type of shoulder.

At such a time the priest will find the following words of Paul the greatest source of inspiration and comfort: "For our wrestling is not against flesh and blood, but against the Principalities and the Powers, against the world-rulers of this darkness, against the spiritual forces of wickedness on high" (Eph. 6:12). These words afford not only comfort and consolation; they offer the key to the divine sense of humor already referred to.

A sense of humor is the ability to see through things and see their funny side. The divine sense of humor, therefore, must be the ability afforded by the "eyes of faith," whereby one can see through the furtive actions of others, and behold the hand of Satan lurking in the background. What on earth could be funnier than that! Yes, what could be funnier than to see Satan impishly striving to obstruct the Almighty's work in the priesthood! Perhaps "ludicrous" is the better word. True, it is serious, yet at the same time it is humorous. This explains how the martyrs could laugh in the very face of death. Isn't it ludicrous to find Satan in opposition of our Lord's priesthood when such terrific odds are against him! Doesn't Jesus give us encouragement when He says: "Do not let your heart be troubled, or be afraid. . . . for the prince of the world [of Satan] is coming, and in me he has nothing" (John 14:27,30); "Take courage, I have overcome the world [of Satan]" (John 16:33)! Yes, the Lord stands by us and strengthens us (II Tim. 4:17), so that we can do all things in Him who strengthens us (Phil. 4:13).

No passage in all Scripture rings with more divine humor, the kind we are now discussing, than Paul's words to his priests at Corinth.

Each year on Sexagesima Sunday we review the "perils of Paul," e.g., "in perils from false brethren, in perils from robbers . . ." (II Cor. 11:21). If one does not watch his diction, he can easily find himself reciting them as "the pearls of Paul."

By reason of the power of suggestion, one will not need be ordained too long until he will have a string of "pearls" all of his own. The first "pearl," a huge one, will be the "perils [pearls] from false brethren."

Hence, unless the young priest has caught on with Paul's inspired sense of humor, he will become very discouraged and melancholy. Indeed, he will recite them over and over to himself, and to no good.

As he thumbs these "pearly" beads, over and over—and which one of us hasn't?—animosity and rancor will rise in the heart, despair in the will, until he is ready to throw in the sponge.

Whereas if he has that sense of divine humor, he will, with Paul, find himself reciting the joyful mysteries of the rosary of suffering, the very beads of which he helped to string. He will then sing, "Each bead a pearl, each pearl a joy, each joy a suffering for his Church, for souls, from Satan's stronghold, to buy." With Her he will be going Her way.

This great sense of divine humor will enable the priest to keep the Lord's command: be most forgetting and forgiving to his fellow man. It will help him to understand the Lord's other words: "Trust not the voice of your enemy forever," that is, Satan, who is the "enemy forever." In this way will he see his offenders merely as unwitting tools in the hands of Satan. He may blame Satan, but not the "tools of Satan."

Much to his chagrin, often these tools of Satan will be those in high places, those who are moved by the "spirit" to "administer discipline to that young fellow," "to clip his wings," "to put him in his place," "to take the wind out of his sails."

All the while, with the best of intentions, these "tools" will glowingly think they are "doing a service to God" (John 16:2); that they are administering justice. It could be they are just testing the young fellow to see if he has it in view of some future big appointment. All bishops aren't dumb.

Little doubt, the good Lord will reward them for their good intentions. Let Paul the humorist capsulize this whole idea: "It is no great thing, then, if his [Satan's] ministers disguise themselves as ministers of justice" (II Cor. 11:14).

When I was a young priest, to my great dismay a gentleman wearing the purple said, "If the priest is an Irishman, to keep him in his place, you must kick him in the shins twice a year. If he is German, once a year will suffice." He never said what should happen if one were Swiss. At any rate, my shins were not the place where I felt the foot. And now I must suppose that I was well deserving of the boot, for the sake of suffering in joy, and joy in suffering.

Speaking of "tools of Satan," I learned early in the priesthood that no layman and no nun ever get chesty with a priest unless from somewhere in the background they are being coached by an envious cleric. This is par for the course, according to Scriptured revelation: "By the envy of the devil, death came into the world; and they that follow him are of his side" (Wisd. 2:24).

Everyone is familiar with the Scripture episode of the so-called sons of Thunder, John and James, together with their own mother's politics and apple polishing (Luke 9:52; Matt. 20:21-22). John never forgot the "rebuke" Jesus gave them: "You do not know of what spirit you are" (Luke 9:55). For, in his First Epistle, John writes: "Believe not every spirit, but test the spirits to see whether they are of God . . . every spirit that severs Jesus, is not of God, but is of Antichrist . . . [who] is already in the world" (I John 4:1 ff.). And oh, how many priests have had their initiative destroyed—which is a "severing of Jesus" (*ibid.*).

What greater joy, then, could a priest have than to know he is Satan's most mortal enemy! What greater joy than to know that this enmity is bound up with, and because of, Christ and Christ's priesthood! What greater joy for the priest than to know that because he follows the Blessed Mother, because of Her purity and chastity, he is bound to be in for a siege against celibacy.

Here, again, let us hearken to the words of the warrior Paul: "Therefore let us also, having such a cloud of witnesses over us, put away every encumbrance and the sin entangling us, and run with patience to the fight set before us; looking towards the author and finisher of faith, Jesus, who for the joy set before him, endured a cross, despising shame, and sits at the right hand of the throne of God. Consider, then, him who endured such opposition from sinners against himself, so that you may not grow weary and lose heart. For you have not yet resisted unto blood in the struggle with sin. And you have forgotten the exhortation that is addressed to you as sons, saying, 'My son, neglect not the discipline of the Lord, neither be thou weary when thou art rebuked by him. For whom the Lord loves, he chastises; and he scourges every son whom He receives.' Continue under discipline." (Heb. 12:1 ff.)

What will happen to the bishops, religious superiors, and pastors of assistants who sit around and wonder how they are going to discipline so-and-so after having listened to complaints without getting the other side of the story!

"Due process" is being called for, and promised today. What will come of it? Will they get it? Or will "they" get their "due" in the "process" of that promised "prompt implementation on the diocesan, provincial and regional levels of well-conceived plans for the greater protection of human rights and freedom within the Church"! (Doc. Serv. Houston, 4-21-69.)

What will come to those superiors who, after prostituting the "secret accusations against the accused, and without investigation, proceed to administer discipline! A bishop once said to a priest concerning such a matter, "I always figure where there is a little smoke there must be some fire." The priest said to him, "Bishop, there is such a thing as artificial smoke." The bishop said, "What is artificial smoke?" And the reply was, "Artificial smoke is slander."

How about those who act upon anonymous letters! One bishop said, "I read them, but pay no attention to them." Surely he was lacking in a knowledge of psychiatry. He should have known anything entering the mind eventually subsides into the subconscious, there to remain forever, to color or to discolor, wittingly or unwittingly, all his future thinking.

Anyone reading this script need not be too astute to realize that its content is colored, and I hope not discolored, by what's in the storehouse of the writer's mind.

When I was a young priest, another bishop gave me this

advice: "Whenever I receive a letter, the first thing I do after opening it is to see who wrote it. If you know who wrote it, you read it with better understanding. But if it is not signed, I throw it into the waste basket at once, without ever reading it. The person who reads an anonymous letter is a bigger damn fool than the fool who wrote it."

This bishop had learned the hard way. When he was a parish priest, some woman, through anonymous letters, smeared him. His own bishop believed the slanders. Time passed on. When that woman came to die she confessed her crime. The confessor demanded of her a signed statement of retraction before he would absolve her. The guilty bishop, then, in order to make restitution, had the slandered priest made a bishop. That was the bishop who advised me about anonymous letters. God love him. He had learned the hard way what someone said: "Must one be charred ere thou can'st limn with him!"

Speaking about "action" without investigation, an old priest many years ago told me the following story. This priest, this pastor, was playing host to the counselors of his own religious order. During an informal after dinner session, with the guests cornering the conversation on how to solve all the ills of the Church and the priesthood, my friend finally threw a bombshell at his guests. "Fathers," he said, "the predominant sin of all superiors is to believe everything they hear about their priests, without first investigating." With one accord the foursome shouted, "No, no. You are wrong. Wrong as can be." With that, my friend, having been shouted down, remained quiet until the following day. This day found my friend driving the Big Four back home to their headquarters. Along the way there was a lull in the conversation. At this point my friend spoke up, still mindful of the rebuke he had received the night before. Here is what he said to them at this time: "Fathers, have you heard the latest? I don't know why I didn't mention this to you before. Our Father Provincial eloped with the Mother Superior." That was a bombshell, to be sure. In unison the Big Four exclaimed, "He did? I always thought he was that kind of a man."

When Pope St. Pius X was a young priest, he was charged by his fellow priests with conniving with the Masons in his territory. The bishop believed it and had the young priest on the carpet. Young Sarto, having more courage than most of us priests in the presence of our bishops, said, "Bishop, put your charges down in writing." According to young Sarto, he never heard any more about it. All Sarto had been doing was being about his Father's business in trying to bring the Masons back to the Church.

The story was narrated by Pius X in his old days to a Capuchin father, who passed it along.

There are those who will say this sort of thing happened many years ago, but does not happen today. It is still happening. Only yesterday a priest was asked by a certain person, concerning a matter of national impact, what could be done to overcome the slander which the bishop had accepted without giving this person a just hearing. It's going on all the time. Who wants to fight his bishop! You lose even when you win.

In the case of Sarto it was his confreres, idle workers, who were envious, and so they reported him to the bishop as a seeming just reason for their inactivity. Sarto went on to become Pope because he had the sense of divine humor which found joy in the priesthood of suffering. He saw the hand of Satan's envy using his accusers for his tools.

If the priest develops and retains the sense of divine humor, he most likely will never become a bishop, or Pope, but he will discover joy in the priesthood amidst suffering. He will lose, for the time being, as did our Lord, but there will be a resurrection, if not in this life, then in the next, for sure.

When one is ordained to the priesthood, he asks, without fully realizing it, for this joy and this suffering. One wonders why the seminarian is not made more fully acquainted with the vicissitudes of his life to come. Christ told His first priests at least about the sufferings and joys, despite the fact that He also said, "Many other things I have to say to you but you cannot bear them now" (John 16:12).

These sufferings will come when one is shifted hither and yon with no good reason extended. They will come when diplomacy speaks out of both sides of its mouth; or when it is so transparent it will seem to say, "Guess how many fish I have in this bag and I will give you both of them."

Joy in the priesthood can never spring from disobedience, as Jesus said about those "who have sat on the chair of Moses. All things, therefore, that they command you observe and do. But do not act according to their works; for they talk but do nothing." (Matt. 23:2-3.) Joy in the priesthood can never come from polishing one's own image, nor spring from wholesale denouncing of the seminary, the bishop, or the pastor, nor ever from complicity in overthrowing the law of celibacy.

Joy in the priesthood shall come only from the Spirit of the Father and the Son. Joy in His fruit (Gal. 5:22). For priests, crucified with Christ, joy in the priesthood is in that Cross of the Lord Jesus, through whom the world (of the devil) is crucified to Him and he to the world (of the devil) (Gal. 6:14, 2:18).

We are priests living not for the sake of criticizing or disobeying our bishop or Pope or pastor, nor even of hoping to become a bishop, Pope, or a pastor. We are living and working to advance the kingdom and thereby save our souls, particularly through obedience and suffering entailed thereby, suffering of the human will, to reap the joy that will surely be forthcoming.

Pope St. Gregory the Great said, when referring to the

Lord of the harvest in what he had to say about the "laborers being few," that He was referring not to the paucity of numbers of workers but to the paucity of actual workers: not to the quantity but to the quality of the workers, who are few.

Since these are the days when the myth is being taken out of so many things, now is surely the time to take the myth out of the myth of all myths: the "busy priest," busy doing mostly nothing that counts.

May obedience be our strong desire in all things, for it is better than sacrifice (I Kings 15:22). The same Pope Gregory said it is as wrong to anticipate the Church as it is to disobey the Church.

Let suffering come. We believe and know that joy will always follow in its wake: joy in the priesthood.

4

The human equation, after original sin, always looms large in the verbiage of men. It always will. Perhaps it would be better or more proper to introduce a finer distinction along this line. Whenever one sins we hear the expression, "well, after all he is only human."

To err is human, but to sin is inhuman: "For all that is not from faith is sin" (Rom. 14:23). Genesis informs us that God allowed Adam to name all the animals (Gen. 2:19), but reserved to Himself the naming of Adam and Eve at the time they were created and constituted in the state of original justice and holiness. God called them "human": "He called *their* name man [*adam*] in the day they were created" (Gen. 5:2).

Since they rated a name no higher than that of "man" (human) when they were in grace, surely when they lost grace they must have become inhuman.

We know that God's original blueprint called for a man, a complete man, a whole man: a man of body and soul, and the soul with its soul-sanctifying grace. The "rebirth" that Jesus speaks of in John (3:3 ff.), therefore, is in apposition with the original "birth" in paradise, but in keeping with His own explanation.

While Baptism removes original sin and makes one "human" again, it does not remit or remove all the consequences of that sin, such as physical death and concupiscence (*fomes peccati*)—those furtive factors of imbalance which readily incline to sin (Rom. 7:8).

These latter might well be called the inhuman tendencies still found in man even after Baptism, which Paul refers to as "the sin that dwells in me" (Rom. 7:7-8,20).

In His Sermon on the Mount, Jesus took notice of these inhuman drives and prescribed accordingly with His eight Beatitudes. These Beatitudes are Christ's revised edition of the old Ten Commandments for His New Testament religion. The Decalogue for the most part is in the negative form. The Beatitudes are put in the positive, together with the promised reward for here and now. Well, therefore, have the Scripture experts acted recently in using the word "Happy" in rendering the word "Blessed" to front each of the Beatitudes. That is, blessed with joy.

Among men today it is most unfortunate that the erroneous impression has gained a hold to the extent that happiness, joy and eternal life are special phenomena that are not to begin until after death. The truth is that these phenomena are meant by God to begin and grow with Baptism, are added to at Confirmation and reach new and greater dimensions in the Order of priesthood. "The kingdom of God consists in justice and peace and joy in the Holy Spirit" (Rom. 14:17).

Mark what Paul has to say on the priesthood: "The sure foundation of God stands firm, bearing this seal: 'The Lord knows who are his' . . . he will be a vessel for honorable use, sanctified and useful to the Lord, ready for every good work. But flee the cravings of youth and pursuing justice, faith, charity and peace with those who call on the Lord from a pure heart." (II Tim. 2:19-22.)

Paul wrote to Timothy about "the cravings of youth." I was young once. So was every priest. If the young priest would ever and anon look through the "eyes of faith" to behold what great gifts God has wrought in him with the sacrament of the priesthood, he would not be crying for relevance with this world's tinsel. He could not allow loneliness to overcome him, nor frustration, to the extent where he would like to shuck himself of every vestige of the priesthood. He need never allow that inferior urge to take over when he already is identified with Christ in very person: "With Christ I am nailed to the cross" (Gal. 2:19).

Since the priest is nailed to the Cross with Christ, why should he ever want to come down from that Cross! Does he not realize that it is Satan who is urging such a decision! Does he not realize that while Christ died "once" upon the Cross, nevertheless that act of redemption must be continued through the sacrifice of the altar to the end of time: "as often as the remembrance of this Victim is celebrated, so often is the work of our Redemption carried on" (Secret of Mass IX Sun. post Pent.).

He should know that the liturgy of the Word is but a preparation for the liturgy of the sacrifice. He should know that the quintessence of the liturgy of the Eucharist consists in the mere consecration of the bread and wine, with a drop of water mingled. He should know with the confection of the sacrament of the altar, there is renewed each and every one of the last words of Jesus upon the Cross (I Cor. 11:26).

Thereby, so to speak, he causes to be repeated Jesus' words of thanks and praise to the Heavenly Father. Hence the word Eucharist, i.e., "Thanks."

"Thank you" to God the Father is of the essence of true worship. Again, the priest ought to know that when he renews the consecration, he makes Jesus say again, so to speak, "Father, forgive them, for they know not what they do" (Luke 23:34). With these potent words the further requirement of genuine worship, that of impetration, is realized.

When the "good thief" went to confession on Calvary and said, "Lord, remember me when thou comest into thy kingdom" (Luke 23:42), and when Jesus replied, "Amen, I say to thee this day thou shalt be with me in paradise" (Luke 23:43), there were initiated the sacraments of the dead, including that of the "ministry of reconciliation" (II Cor. 5: 18). In fact, all the sacraments draw their efficacy from the Cross. "Paradise" for the good thief began pronto in his own soul with the divine indwelling.

In the very next words on the Cross, the Lord set the stage for the sacrificial work of propitiation and expiation: "My God, my God, why hast thou forsaken me? . . . I thirst" (Matt. 27:46; John 19:28). In those words our dear Lord is announcing that He is undergoing the very pains of hell so that sinful mankind, personally, will not have to undergo them, if it repents. What pains? The pain of loss and the pain of sense. Of the pains of sense we are told there is none greater than that of thirst.

Since Jesus is God, and therefore infinite, in a moment of time is He able to expiate the debt of an eternal hell for men's deserving sins.

The pain of loss is that everlasting despair of ever seeing and being with God in His heaven, and for whom we were created. To be forsaken by one's own Father, and in this case God our Father, must truly be hell.

The pain of sense is the pain of that everlasting fire fitted to the person of the unrepentant sinner—much as the human body is fitted to the human soul, so shall fire be fitted to the soul of those "whose portion shall be in the pool that burns with fire and brimstone" (Apoc. 21:8).

When Jesus said, "I thirst," He was announcing that He was redeeming us from that everlasting thirst in hell—the thirst so dramatically portrayed by the "rich man and Lazarus" in Luke (16:19 ff.). What greater joy could there be than that of the priesthood! Just to think the thought faith affords! The priest, with Jesus, becomes victim for the people so that they may suitably worship God the Father. What Jesus did upon the Cross is not yet what man has done. Jesus' sacrifice of thanks, praise, impetration, propitiation, and expiation is the form of worship demanded by God the Father. It furnishes mankind with God's own designed, instituted, and approved official action of worship. This worship, the priest is "obliged to offer for sins, as on behalf of the people, so also for himself" (Heb. 5:3). Paul tells us, "Jesus . . . suffered death, that by the grace of God he might taste death for all" (Heb. 2:9), including both the first and the "second death," or hell.

If ever Satan was able to deceive some of the people of God, it is surely today. "Divide and conquer" always has been his mode of attack. He is at it now through divisiveness in the matter of celibacy. One reads where some who are caught in his nets are saying that priesthood is not a sacrament of Orders, and so they hurry into Matrimony to get their "orders."

Pope Paul VI has given us a beautiful and positive exposé on celibacy. What need be there for saying anything further! However, there is a word or two not touched on by Pope Paul.

It has always been a point of concern on my part to wait for the very first statement from a newly elected Pope. "From the abundance of the heart the mouth speaketh." Pius XI, so far as I was able to ascertain from the news media at the time, made this initial statement before his installation as Pope: "It is proxima Fidei that the Pope should always reside in Rome." Strange as it may seem, that statement seems to have been lost on every periodical at the time.

If it is "proxima Fidei" for the Pope to reside at Rome, and I believe it, since Pius XI so said, then surely it must also be proxima Fidei that the Roman clergy be celibate.

Many of the writers today are saying that most of the Apostles were married men; and that Paul said a bishop should be a husband of only one wife (I Tim. 3:2,12). Now, it cannot be proved that the Apostles were for the most part, married men. And suppose they were; so what!

We must be understanding. When Jesus was on earth, the span of life's expectancy was less than twenty-three years. People married very young by our standards. Witness the Blessed Mother at the age of fourteen or younger.

Our Lord needed priests. Where was He to get them? He couldn't select little unmarried boys and wait for them to grow up, so He did the best thing under the circumstances. He selected the elders or oldsters, as we say today. Hence when the Scriptures were done in Greek and Latin (see James 5:14), they used the only word they had, namely *presbyteros,* meaning elder. The elders became the priests, and the priests were the elders. That it was imperative to select married men is rather evident from Paul's advice to Timothy about a bishop's being "a husband of only one wife." This is not to say that Timothy was a married man. But it is to say that if Timothy was constrained to impose hands on a married man, and his wife died, then he was not to remarry. This conclusion is warranted from Paul's strong advice to widows and to the unmarried: ". . . it is good for them if they so remain, even as I" (I Cor. 7:8). While there is no positive ordinance from the Lord on the subject, neither is there any positive statement concerning slavery. Our Lord never spoke positively against slavery. Yet He could not have been in favor of it. He knew it would take centuries to form the consciences of the new Christians universally on the matter. You don't change people overnight. The case for celibacy can be made stronger than that for slavery when referring to the silence of Scripture.

While our Lord did not make celibacy of the essence of the priesthood, yet He did have something to say on the matter. He knew if He had made celibacy of the essence of the priesthood, neither He nor the Church at that time would have had much of a priesthood, as to numbers.

However, He did make Himself pretty clear on what His expectations were regarding celibacy, while remaining silent on the matter of slavery.

After our Lord had forbidden divorce, with remarriage, the disciples showed considerable knowledge of sex psychology by saying: "If the case of a man with his wife is so, it is not expedient to marry" (Matt. 19:10). The disciples were understanding to the extent that once one has indulged the sex appetite, it would be rough not to be able to continue in marriage after a divorce. They quickly drew the conclusion: "it would not be expedient to marry." The expedient thing would be to practice continency from the outset. This information should be set forth to the seminarians today who are permitted to have dates in order to see if they have a vocation in the priesthood. How silly can we get!

Our Lord must have been discussing marriage in relation to the priesthood on this occasion, for His disciples. For He went on to say: "Not all can accept this teaching; but those to whom it has been given. For there are eunuchs who were born so from their mother's womb; and there are eunuchs who are so made by men; and there are eunuchs who have made themselves so for the sake of the kingdom of heaven. Let him accept it who can." (Matt. 19:10-12.)

Surely Our Lord's silence on slavery thrown against His articulateness on celibacy shows that celibacy loomed very large in His wishes, at that very time, difficult though it would be.

The Church bided Her time in preparing Her priests against the day when celibacy would become a universal law. It was not until St. Gregory the Great (590-604) that the law of celibacy became law universally. And it was not until another five hundred years that St. Gregory VII (1073-85), better known as Hildebrand, revived the same law. However, through the centuries the Church through private councils, and in particular dioceses, always worked towards that end. But the matter of slavery has not been resolved, even to this day, 100 per cent.

May the present law of celibacy never be voided. Rather, let us keep in mind that Jesus was a virgin; and that so was John, who served at the altar of the Mass of the Cross. And so was the Blessed Mother, who was co-celebrant or co-redemptrix at the Mass of the Cross.

Little wonder that Jesus stated His preference in favor of celibacy in His disquisition with the disciples as quoted above from Matthew. He desired a priesthood that would give itself undividely to His Heavenly Father as He had done; and "the disciple is not above the Master."

One of the sacrificial statements in the liturgy of the Word and the liturgy of the sacrifice of the Cross was: "Woman, behold, thy son." [Son], "Behold, thy mother" (John 19:26). These words were not spoken to John as John. They were spoken to the "disciple," who was a priest, a celibate priest. This is to say there was that new dimension of the supernatural order, which is celibacy.

Jesus was celibate. Mary was celibate. John was celibate. There was present the nucleus for His celibate priesthood in the sanctuary of Golgotha. That nucleus was to grow. And it did grow. So after centuries it had taken on such proportions that it became law—because the Church then was strong enough to withstand the shock of any dissidents who might not go along with the law of celibacy.

The Church today, in America, is also strong enough to withstand any shock forthcoming from dissidents whose superficial claims are inspired and prompted by the Evil One.

Suffice it to add, there would be more sins in this country with a married priesthood than there are now with a celibate priesthood. Ask the doctors who treat diseases. Satan is always busy. Besides, the very disciples quoted in Matthew agreed a married priesthood would not be expedient, as we saw above.

Such is the supreme joy in the priesthood. All the powers of hell and earth must not separate us from that joy in the Lord.

It is not the law of celibacy that needs to be changed. It is the unwritten law that prohibits the teaching of modesty, purity, and chastity, lest one be accused of teaching sex, and be scolded by his bishop.

This teaching would be the proper kind of preparation both for marriage and for the priesthood. Then at the proper age let them decide which road to follow.

An Englishman who returned after a lecture tour in America was asked at the pier what his impressions were of America. He quickly answered, "The Americans wear the fig leaf only over their mouths."

Years ago a priest lectured a large group of nuns on how to teach children a knowledge of all the virtues. When the virtues of purity and chastity came up for discussion, there was standing room only. Before taking up each virtue of purity and chastity a quiz was had: "What is purity?" The most that came from any of the nuns was that purity is water that contains no germs, or the sky that is free from pollution.

After the lecture was finished, a real old nun came up and spoke as follows: "I want to shake your hand. I have been mistress of postulants in our community for thirty-five years. You, today, taught me for the first time the meaning of those words, including virginity."

Most priests have had married women say, "If someone had explained to me the meaning of those virtues, I would gladly have gone to the convent." How can we have a happy priesthood and sisterhood and joy in the Lord when they have not been properly prepared for it!

PART TWO

5

Fr. Kathy, what are you so excited about?

Kathy. Is it O.K. to kill little babies before they are born?

Fr. That is something to be excited about. Let me ask you: Is it O.K. to kill little babies after they are born?

Kathy. I heard them talking on TV about it. I think they called it abortion. What is that?

Fr. To abort something means to do away with it on purpose, not by accident; in this case long before the baby gets a full start in its mother's womb.

For example, it takes several weeks or months for a baby to get a good, strong start in growth in its mother cradle of flesh, called her womb, which is lower down than her heart and tummy. Ask your mother to explain.

Remember how Gabriel and St. Elizabeth sang to Mary: "Blessed is the fruit of your womb." They were referring to the baby Jesus, who was in the sanctuary of the Blessed Virgin Mary's womb, in her cradle of flesh.

That is where Christ was ordained High Priest and anointed with the "oil of gladness" when the divine nature of the Word united with His human nature in the one divine person of the Son of God.

God the Son, the second person of the Blessed Trinity, came from heaven and entered Mary's womb. Of course, the Father and Holy Spirit came too, because the three persons are one God, as we believe and know.

That was the day the archangel Gabriel told or announced to Mary that such a mysterious thing was going to happen, and did happen (Luke).

After being sure it was not a false angel in the person of Satan, Mary then said, "Be it done to me according to your word."

All this happened by the "power of the Holy Spirit," as St. Luke reported it.

Almost ever since, Catholics have remembered and celebrated that day as the Feast of the Annunciation, on March 25.

Since Mary took the vow of virginity when She was a little girl, the Archangel Gabriel's message put Mary ill at ease. How could She give Her body to someone else when She already had promised Her soul and body to God alone! No one else, not even Herself, would ever tamper with the body She had promised. She would share it with no one. Such was Her promise in Her vow of virginity.

Mary also understood that Her baby, who was to be the Son of God, and was to be called Jesus, would both enter Her body and leave it, after nine months, without ever opening the door thereto, by the miraculous power of God.

The day He would be born would be and was called Christmas. Her virginity would remain intact before, during, and after, and forever.

We celebrate Christmas in the United States as Jesus' birthday. This does not mean that He is born each year on Christmas. It means that each year after that is the anniversary of his birthday. He died at thirty-three. That leaves Him still thirty-three, because there is no time or age in heaven.

Everyone wonders how Jesus could be born without opening the door in Mary's body. Catholics believe it because the Bible says so and the Church teaches so. Some other people do not believe it at all. This is because they do not properly understand who God is or how Mary is His mother.

For example, a couple of years ago a woman said to me, "I always give Mary my sympathy on Christmas. I myself gave birth to several children, and what a hard time I had! I can appreciate fully what Mary had to suffer."

Little did she believe or realize what took place. She did not believe that Mary was a virgin before the birth, during the birth, and after the birth. If this woman only knew Mary is suffering because so many people will not honor Her! For those who have to have an explanation some put it this way.

On Easter Sunday, the Bible says, Jesus, after rising from the dead (grave), came and stood in the midst of the Apostles, "the doors being closed [bolted] for fear of the Jews" (John 20:19). Why fear? They were afraid they would be put to death also, because they identified with Jesus.

If you ask, "How did Jesus get into the womb?" then they say, "Well, that is what the Bible says, and I believe what is in the Bible."

The way He got into that room without opening the door was the same way He got through the door to Mary's cradle when He first entered and when He was born nine months later without opening the door.

God can do anything He wants to do. Since that baby Jesus was and is God and at the same time a baby man, as God He sort of penetrated everything in His way so He could enter or leave without opening the door.

We must never say, "How?" to God. He can do anything, everything. That is how He got the name of God in the Bible. The Bible tells us the word God means "all-powerful."

To destroy a little baby at any time before it is big enough or strong enough to live outside its mother's womb "in the air" (viable) is to do an abortion. Any time after that, for one to destroy the little baby in the womb is first-class murder.

I saw a little baby once at a hospital that had fallen out of its mother's cradle when it was, they said, two weeks old (some would dispute this age because of its size.)

It was preserved in a jar containing formaldehyde. It was about the size of a honeybee and shaped like the opposite end of a honeybee on the end where the legs and feet are. That is to say, that part of the body from the waist down was not yet developed. The head and arms and fingers were very noticeable. The eyes were open and blue in color—real blue.

That part of the body from the waist down was round like a filled sack of wheat or as I said, like the bottom of a honeybee.

Kathy. Is that the way Jesus got His start in Mary's womb?

Fr. Exactly; only He never fell out, or was forced out, of His mother's womb. He came out at the proper time by a miracle.

As we celebrate it today in the words of St. John in the Bible: "The Word was made flesh," on the 25th of March, and on Christmas "dwelt among men." He was not born like other children, as described above.

To be born means "to be brought out into life or existence." Jesus came out on His own. You see, He is God. His God nature (divine nature) overcame His human nature so that He could come out without destroying or injuring either His own or His Mother's body. That left Her a virgin. Other mothers do not have it that way. Ask your own mother or father if you want to know more about it. But don't ask anyone else. It is too sacred to talk about among other kids. It is nothing to snicker about either. You wouldn't snicker about Jesus and Mary or your own mother, would you?

Kathy, you said you heard them speaking about abortion on TV. I have also so heard. You know what? Of late, they are giving everyone a "big hand" who on TV say they are about to have a baby or did have one or several children in the past.

Then they are crying about soldier boys dying in war, whether big boys or men are killed in Vietnam or little babies, what's the difference? Size does not make one inhuman. See! It is a lack of God's indwelling.

Someone said it is far more human to have your baby on your lap than on your conscience.

Those who are so doing today, according to the media, will, in fifteen years or so, be fit candidates for mental institutions.

Some parents are too shy when it comes to speaking about having children. It is their duty. Many are behind the times. They always have been on this particular subject.

Their kids know all about it from other kids before even they start to school. This from other and older children, some of whom are not so good. As I heard a man say on TV today, "No, I'm not married. I won't be until I find someone that is real good." However, he said, "I don't mind dating one that I know is not good."

The trouble is, these little ones think they know something their parents don't know. In this way they can and often do get into trouble. Children should never be left alone, nor should they be permitted to go visit their grandparents or relatives away from home. They will not get the proper supervision.

This stuff is usually handed down by some one two years their elders. And so false knowledge and practice trickle down from oldsters to all others below them.

The following story illustrates what was just said. One day two mothers were walking down the street past a zoo. They had two little girls walking in front of them. Finally one little girl turned and said, "Oh, Mother, look at those large birds. What are they?"

One of the mothers answered, "Those are storks. They are the birds that bring babies into the world."

At that the other little girl said, "Oh, the poor dumb things! Let's go and tell them differently."

Susan. How come parents can hardly wait until they get their new babies baptized?

Fr. Whenever a child is born into this world, excepting Jesus and Mary, it comes deprived of sanctifying grace. This is to say that the Blessed Trinity, the three persons in one God—God the Father, God the Son, and God the Holy Spirit —are not living in that child.

You ought to know that when God created our first parents, commonly called Adam and Eve, they were in their very beginning, the very temple or dwelling, home or house, of God. That was why God created them. He did it this way so they could love God in their very own temple which they were then, right from the start.

However, the devil came along and could see that God was dwelling in them. That made the devil envious because he, the devil, wanted them for his own house. So the devil tempted them. The devil got them to forget about God and to believe in the devil which they did. They "ate up" everything the devil told them. It got so bad that God had to leave their temple, or souls, as we say today.

So now, when children are born into the world they are born without God in their temple. They belong to the devil's kingdom.

That sin which Adam and Eve committed was called the original sin, because it had its origin with them. Thus it is that everyone is born in the state of original sin.

Even Mary, the Blessed Virgin, was due by the law of heredity, to be born in the state of original sin, but God made Her an exception. He did this so that when Jesus would be born of Her, He, as man, would not inherit the state of original sin. He did this because, as God, Jesus was above and before all angels and man.

The exception God made in Mary's case is called Her Immaculate Conception, as She called it Herself when She appeared to little Bernadette at Lourdes in 1854.

The word conception means a "beginning." When Mary began it was as a tiny infant smaller yet than that honeybee we spoke about. Mary began in the cradle of flesh in Her mother Ann's body. And of course She loved God the Father, Son and Holy Spirit, who were in Her temple, so much that She never ever committed even a venial sin.

She loved God, and God loved her.

This original-sin business was believed already in the Old Testament. In the Book of Psalms we read, "In sin did my mother conceive me." That is the short (figurative) way of saying, "In the state of sin did my mother conceive me."

Some erroneously conclude from that short text that conception is a sin. If it were, then God would be guilty of sin because He is the one who creates the soul so that conception can happen.

Steve. One hears a lot about how to baptize: whether by pouring or by immersion.

Fr. Thank you. That's a honey.

In the Bible two kinds of Baptism are recorded: the one, that of St. John the Baptist, "unto repentance"; the other, that of Jesus, "unto everlasting life."

John's baptism was in peparation for the coming of Jesus. It did not confer the grace of God, but prepared or disposed or got the people ready in mind and heart to receive Jesus' baptism.

Jesus' baptism, He brought from heaven. It took away sins and prepared the soul to be the temple of God and to receive God as one's guest; and it also makes one a member of the Church, as St. Paul writes to the Corinthians (I Cor. 12:13 ff.).

The Bible speaks of St. John baptizing in the river Jordan. So, naturally, since most people think with the help of their imaginations, most suppose John had to immerse them.

In the United States whenever we refer to a river we picture a deep stream of water that is over a man's head.

In those days they were hard up for words, so they called any flowing stream of water a river. Whether it would be a real river, or a stream or a creek, or a brook, or a rivulet or a trickle of water, it was nonetheless called a river. So, since John baptized in the river Jordan, the only place where for miles around there was any flowing water to be had, people in our country suppose John immersed them.

You want to hear a good story? O.K.

Years ago I was driving out in the country to visit some non-Catholics who had invited me to their home. They gave me the directions on a piece of paper. It must have been twenty miles, more or less. When I came to the end of the written instructions, it appeared that I had come almost to the end of the road. I saw a small cottage at the side of the road and decided the smart thing to do was to go there and inquire in order not to get stuck in the mud.

A gentleman opened the door. After telling me to go a little further, he said in astonishment, "You look like a minister." I said, "No, I look like a priest, which I am." "Are you a priest?" he exclaimed. "Won't you come in, please? You are the first priest I ever saw." "I'm happy for such an honor," said I. "I promised myself if I ever met a Catholic priest, I would set him and the Catholic Church straight on Baptism," he said. "There must be millions of Catholics all over the world. Few are ever baptized by immersion. That's the only right way. So you set your church right on this point."

I said, "Thank you for your kindness. What is the source of your information?" He said, "The Bible says John baptized Jesus in the river Jordan by immersion."

I said, "Sir, do you have a Bible?" He said, "Sir, you insult me by asking me if I, a minister, have a Bible." I said, "I mean you no insult, sir. To me it is a worse insult to have a Bible and never to have read it than not to have one. Please get your Bible and read it out loud." At this he went into another room for the Bible. He looked and looked for

Jesus' baptism and finally said, "I can't find it now." He was nervous. So I said, "Look in Matthew 3:16." This he did and read, ". . . forthwith he came up from the water."

The minister, having read otherwise than he spoke, said, "By jinx, it doesn't say that, does it? But it means that."

You know what? Here is one for Ripley, believe it or not. All the while I was facing the gentleman I was looking at a picture hanging on the wall behind the chair upon which he sat. What do you suppose that picture turned out to be? It showed John and Jesus standing in the river Jordan with the water barely trickling over their feet. The Baptist held a clamshell in his hand and was pouring water on Jesus' head.

Even if John did immerse Jesus, that was John's baptism and unrelated to the first and most necessary of the seven sacraments instituted by our Lord to prepare absolutely for God's other six different kinds of grace, which are Confirmation, Holy Eucharist, Penance, Holy Anointing, Holy Orders (rank), and Matrimony.

If immersion were essential rather than pouring of water, then to be the most effective, one should be baptized in the Pacific Ocean because it has the deepest water.

Sacraments are mental signs, and if you understand the meanings of the signs, you will know what takes place. God understands because He gave those signs their meaning.

In Baptism the pouring or immersion with water is a sign of cleansing, refreshment, and admittance to a new life in the Church. It effects absolutely what is signified. The very sign asks for that effect.

The little boy who shakes his fist at another little boy is asking for it—a fight, I mean—as all understand.

Take for instance in war. We are told that in the older days when one side wished to surrender, a white flag was hoisted. That was the sign of surrender, but that cause did not necessarily effect the stop of fighting.

In Baptism we place the sign in the name of the Trinity, and the Trinity, understanding its sign, moves into the soul so soon as it sees this sign.

When Jesus was baptized He needed no grace from John's baptism because He, together with the Father and the Spirit, are the Trinity: three in one God.

Here let me tell you a good story on how clever the devil is. One night I was hearing confessions. There was a lull. Finally some woman came into the church. A light hung in front of the "box" so people could read their prayer books. When this woman came into the box, I started to mumble in Latin this prayer which today goes in English thus: "May God be in your heart and upon your lips so that you may truthfully and properly confess all of your sins, in the name of the Father and of the Son and of the Holy Ghost." As I began the mumbling of that prayer, the woman left the box and pulled the drop cord on the light. There was complete darkness. I asked the woman upon her return why she did that. She replied, "I heard you say, 'Put the light out.' How by any stretch of the imagination could one turn Latin words into English! Now you know why the Church has holy water in the front of all churches. Now you know why certain people hear things in the sermon the priest never said and never thought of saying. So use the drop of holy water as you enter church with great faith and devotion. The old boy just could be riding on your shoulder. No, this is not superstition. How well Satan would so like you to think!

A priest once told me this story. He thought he was sitting all alone in the church, yet inside the box. After a while this priest heard a sound as if someone else was in the box. So the priest said several times, "Go ahead with your confession." Nothing happened. So the priest went into that side of the box. There stood a funny-looking man. "What are you doing here?" exclaimed the priest. The answer came, "I am the devil. I take fear out of people in order to get them to sin. Now I am here to put fear in them so they will be afraid to make a good confession." Yes, I know you will shout, "Square!" but always remember that hell is up to date.

St. Francis of Assisi's former prayer contained the line "Lord help me to be understanding rather than to be understood." Cardinal Merry del Val, secretary to St. Pius X, had in his breviary a card with these words found after his death: "Lord, let me be misunderstood." I never had to pray to be misunderstood. The children understood but not all the oldsters once "civilization" finally caught up with them. I had particular love and patience for children because they thought of God and themselves until civilization caught up with them also—then, like all of us oldsters they did think mostly of self as witnessed by these two stories:

A little girl standing in front of a window said during a storm, "Oh, Mamma, God just took my picture." And the little boy was heard to say as the father passed by his bedroom door at his night prayers, "Dear God, bless Daddy and Mother, but don't send them any more children; they don't know how to take care of the one they now have." I agree. People know more about raising crops, flowers, and gardens, and making money, than about child psychology.

Now, let us get on with the story of experiences you resurrected from the past fifty years.

In speaking of understanding it was always my policy to be understanding. In order to do this one had to be a good listener. I don't know how many times those who rang the doorbell went away with these words on their lips: "Thanks for listening, anyway." I may have learned it from my mother always to hear people out. If they can only unburden their souls of whatever bothers them, that in itself is a big help.

Bob. How did you come to hit upon dialogue as the best way to impart knowledge?

Fr. Let me tell you a good story. The very first parish I was appointed to brought it about in this way.

Religion class was scheduled for the first time on some appropriate day agreeable to all the youngsters, probably a Saturday, when they were not at school or a Sunday so they might go with Papa and Mama. Believe it or not, none of the kiddies in all eight grades came up with an answer excepting one little girl. When asked to recite the Hail Mary, finally in desperation, in order to get some kind of reply, only Susie held up her hand. Her father had a fruit market. Thus did she begin: "Hail Mary, full of grapes, etc." I was wild on the inside, but to this day I am still proud of myself for holding my cool. When class was over I sat down alone with my thoughts and said, "Come, Holy Ghost." At once this thought came into my mind: "If the kids knew the answers, they would not need you." You are the one to know the answers. Let them ask you the questions. The very next class after a prayer to the Holy Ghost (so called in those days) class started thus: "Well, children, what would you like to know? Ask me anything that is on your minds that has to do with religion." Perhaps the stiffest one was, "Where or what makes twins?"

Mark. How old must a child be until it can make its first Holy Communion?

Fr. The law of the Church reads: if possible, after Confirmation, as soon as a child has the use of reason.

Now you will want to know when the use of reason comes. Some children are brighter than others. In a word, as soon as a child knows what it is doing.

For example: "Early one evening I called on a family to see if they needed help. Mamma said to Pat (5 years old), "Show Father how you can say your prayers." To my heart's content Pat said, "It ain't time to go to bed yet."

I said "to my heart's content" because that is one of my worst pet peeves: to have parents or teachers make their children show off by reciting their prayers. It takes the love of God out of it.

Another time Grandpa was talking to a crowd standing around him, including a six-year-old grandchild. As he turned he accidentally scuffed her foot because he did not notice her. Grandpa said, "Excuse me, God bless you" as he patted her on the head. Martha replied, "I didn't sneeze." That was good reasoning, which is understanding the relation between cause and effect.

Speaking of children and their prayers, these can already be learned and said in family devotions at home, preferably before an image of Jesus or Mary, when a child is four years old. It has been done. It is done. No need for exhibition. They learn fast.

Judy. Some people like it and some don't, now that you have no solemn First Communion. How come you don't have solemn First Communion?

Fr. Receiving Holy Communion for the first time is solemn enough without a parade of new clothes. The same holds for the second, third, etc., communions. People should not be averse to change. Why not keep abreast of the times? We need not live in the days of the oxcart.

Many years ago I read a book by a certain cardinal. In this book the cardinal was telling how Pope St. Pius X, about 1905, said children should make their First Communion as soon as they have the use of reason. He used some strong words. He said, when a child is ripe for it he can learn in five minutes all that one needs to know in order to receive Jesus.

He even went farther and said that even if a child should slide back mentally, a little, so as "to lose his taste for Holy Communion, now and then, he could wait until such a period of time elapsed until he desires to communicate with his Lord again."

You want to know something?

Class. What?

Fr. One day just before Christmas, I called at a home on business. As I was about to leave, with overcoat and hat on, the mother said, "Father, Janey [6 years old] has been pestering me about receiving her First Communion. How about it? She's too young. She does not know enough." I replied, "There is no time like the present." I sat down; put Janey on my knee; turned her back to her mother so she could not read the answers to my questions off her mother's face. Then I started to find out if she was "ripe" or not.

When I had finished, I said, "Of course you know enough." Then I said to the mother, "Could you have answered all of those questions?" Her mother said, "I'm afraid not." The mother still urged her point by saying, "But, Janey, you have no new dress." With that Janey, in tears of joy at the thought of soon communicating, stamped her foot on the floor and said, "I don't want a new dress. I just want to receive Jesus."

Now, what do you say, class? The mother was not too strong a Catholic then. She seemed to lean toward her non-Catholic husband's way: indifference. He came around, though, some years later, maybe because of Janey's prayers.

Another time I stopped at a home. The quickest entrance to the house was through the side door to the kitchen. There the mother and I sat and chatted, or better, I listened. Finally that mother said, "Father, Dawn [5 years old] is asking all the time when she might make her First Communion." Again I used my famous slogan: "No time like the present. Where is Dawn?" "She is in the front room watching TV," came the reply. "O.K., call her out. It won't take long to find out if she knows enough."

Among other questions I asked Dawn why she wished to

receive Communion. She replied, "So I can love Jesus like I do my mamma and papa." With that I let her down from my knee and said to the mother, "Now, do you think she knows enough?" St. Thomas Aquinas could not have said it better, if as well, when he was five or six. She made her First Communion the next time they went to Mass and is always so present to this day.

Instead of showing off their children by regimentation, I ask the whole family relationship to honor the child and our Lord by communicating at the same time. This is far better than the way they used to do when all the children marched in together the same day, with the oldsters taking pictures and abstaining from Communion and everyone conscious of their new clothes.

Dawn really set the record straight. She said "so I can love Jesus," etc., that is, so she could give herself to Jesus. The rest of us always speak of receiving Him, which is not real sharp so far as love goes, because love wants to give. We give ourselves to Jesus; He gives Himself to us.

Every year or so I take all the children when they are older and let them make their solemn Communion in a group as the old-timers used to call it. Their mind then is not on their clothes so much as on Jesus.

The next time I saw Dawn's mother she told me she was bothered by her women friends (whose 7-year-olds had not received) who kept saying, "How can you allow it? She does not know enough."

To this I replied, "Will you be shocked at my answer?" She assured me she wouldn't. Then I said, "You ask your friends if each of them, man or woman, when they came to get married, didn't bargain for a virgin. Jesus wants virgin-pure souls for His first guests in Communion."

Maybe you do not know it, but if one never commits a mortal sin, such a one would never have to go to confession.

Parents are overanxious to have their babies baptized. Why not be anxious to have them make their First Communion?

I'm not recommending such procedure concerning confession, however. You know, such little tikes have such delicate consciences that a small venial sin seems a mountainous mortal sin to them. Love is delicate, you know. If that ever happens, some few years after their First Communion, they'll be smart enough to ask for confession.

That is why I tell parents to take their little children over to church to have a good look in the box (confessional) so they get an idea of what the oldsters are going in and out about.

Every doctor's office is filled on specified days when children are to come and get their shots against different diseases. The same should hold for us in confession.

It delights my ears to hear persons come into the box and say, "Bless me, Father, for I have sinned. I am a little girl or boy or man or woman so many years old. I'm happy to say I have no new sins; I just came to get the grace [antitoxin] for my old sins."

Also, the little ones should be told, several times till they learn how to confess, to say also, "Father, please help me out. This is my first [or second or third confession]." Such is being human. Such is the way Jesus would do it, and the priest represents Jesus in person or is supposed to. For such was he ordained to the priesthood.

6

Luke. What does "venial sin" mean?

Fr. The word "venial" itself applies to a sin that is easily forgiven. That is why they are advocating global confession, or global absolution, today for venial sins. But keep in mind, I am not. There is no substitute for the sacrament of Penance. Remember that! It is thrilling to have Jesus as one's guest.

What sins do children usually commit?

Class. Telling lies and disobeying.

Fr. I thought you'd say that. Listen! Most of the acts of disobedience are not even a sin at all. Not, unless, in some way they are hooked up with one of the Ten Commandments. For example, if your mother tells you to close that door or to get up off the floor, etc., etc., etc., and you do not heed her, that would be no sin at all in itself.

The best way to find out is to ask your mother or father when they tell you to do something, "Is that an order?" If they say, "Yes," then of course some little sin would be connected with the disobedience.

Especially would this be true if they said, "You be home at ten o'clock—that's a tall order." Then that sounds serious. You see, your parents work hard all day and are tired. All you do is play. Isn't it enough for them to sleep with one eye open, tired as they are, waiting for you to come home?

Then, about lies. There are two kinds: lies of defense and lies of offense. If you tell a lie because you are thinking of avoiding a few stings on your behind, that is a defensive lie. But if you tell a lie to hurt someone seriously, that is an offensive lie and can be serious depending on what it is about, or how malicious it is.

John. Father, did you ever whip a child or anyone?

Fr. Yes—only once. This is good—listen! Normally I do not believe in it.

A mother and her twelve-year-old boy were at odds. Mother and father were separated, whether because of work in another state or because of trouble, I'll never know. I was too polite to ask her, and she did not say. Anyway, the mother was not a Catholic, and she said, "I'm a woman; this boy is too big for me to whip. He's bigger than I am, you know. Whenever I tell him what to do, he gets mean and says, 'I'm going to commit suicide.'

"So that is why we are here. You take this stick, Father; I authorize you to give this boy a good licking with it in my place." This was the first and last time such ever happened to me.

So what else could I do but proceed to give him a (light) licking? When I had finished, he said, "Now I'm going to kill myself." At that I said, "You haven't had enough yet, eh?" Then I gave him a real good one.

Some weeks later he was back to see me and was O.K. He was cured. Halfway measures never succeed, even in whippings. Years later, after he had grown to maturity, he came and thanked me for doing what I had done.

Outside of that instance I have never whipped or touched a child. My appeal, no matter what wrong they did, was to say, "Go and be a lady [or a gentleman]." Then I forgot about it. That appeal was always successful. That is the way Jesus did it: "Go, sin no more," He said.

Pat. How did you get that way?

Fr. Well, you know, when I went to boarding school, all of us were constantly being punished, lots of times when we did not know what for. One of the prefects (so those in charge were called) used to get up in the top of a tree to spy on and to catch the young boys who were smoking. I vowed then and there (although I never smoked at that time), "None of that stuff for me." That's not being a gentleman. Kids will hate you.

You want to know something? O.K. For three years I was stationed at an orphans' villa. The sisters were in charge. One day three of them cornered me and said, "Father, you are so successful with the children, won't you please let us read the books you have on child psychology?"

I said, "I'm sorry, I have only one; but I can't let you have it." "Oh, please, we'll take good care of it and bring it back."

"It is my little red notebook—my brain, my memory, my mind. I can't give that to you. Sisters," I said, "if I have any success with children, it is because I treat them as I wished to have been treated when I was a child." That's what Jesus, the divine psychologist, said: "Do to others as you would like to be done by" or some such words. I always promised never to do the fool things to others that were done to me; and I was no saint when I was a kid.

You know, speaking of orphans makes me think of a good one that is often in the question columns today: people asking why women don't wear hats in church, and if it is wrong. Well, you get as many different answers as you have persons writing. Most of them are in error.

The present law of the Church reads: "The woman should assist [participate] in modest dress and with heads covered, especially when they approach the Table of the Lord (Canon 1262).

The Church never gives reasons for her laws. We all know that St. Paul says: "Judge for yourselves: does it become a woman to pray to God uncovered? Does not nature itself teach you that for a man to wear his hair long is degrading; but for a woman to wear hers long is a glory to her? Because her hair has been given her as a covering. But if anyone is disposed to be contentious—we have no such custom, neither have the churches of God." (I Cor. 11:13-17.)

I believe everything, anything, in the Bible, if properly reported, as St. Augustine once said. If I don't understand what the Bible means when it says something, then I study about it till I find out what it means.

When I read what St. Paul said about women covering their heads, I wondered what he meant. It dawned on me one day that really a woman is not dressed up unless she wears a head covering, or better, a hat. I recalled my own mother's actions when, in my boyhood, we were getting ready to go to church. If my mother was all ready to leave and she had her hat on, she would sit down and wait for the rest of us (which was not very often). She never did another lick after she had her hat on. But when she didn't have her hat on yet, she went about the house doing this and that. But if she had her hat on, then she was relaxing, sedate-like, because she was fully dressed, lady-like.

That taught me that unless and until a woman had her hat on she was not 100 per cent in an inactive stage. When she went to church or anyplace else, she was all dressed up if she had her hat on. Her attitude was that of a lady so far as her actions were concerned. (This is not to say she would not be a lady otherwise.)

For example, it also dawned on me that if I hauled some woman to the depot or to the hospital or, any place, those seeing a woman in the auto with me would think or say, "I wonder where Father is taking that lady." They would make nothing of it. But if the same woman did not have a hat on, or head covered, or was bareheaded, as they say, and people would see us together they would think or say to themselves, "Oh! Oh!" They would imagine the worst.

One day the superior of the orphans' villa consulted me. Said she, "Have you not noticed how talkative the girls are in church?"

I said, "Have I? You know, I can hardly say Mass because of the distractions."

"What can be done about it?" inquired the superior. Have you a solution?"

"Yes," said I. "I can cure it in five minutes."

"What's the cure?" she asked.

I said, "Put hats on them. When a girl or woman has a

hat on, she is fully dressed like a lady. They are more reserved and not so mettlesome. They are on their good behavior." Hats they wore after that, and the cure was instant.

Linda. What do you think about little girls having their beaus?

Fr. It isn't what I think. It is what God or after Him anyone should think. It is a terrible thing. Remember how angry Jesus got about teaching little children scandal? The word "scandal" comes from some such word that used to mean to stumble into sin.

It may seem cute when they are little tots. It won't be near so cute when those same little ones become teenagers and make their mothers become grandmothers before they become mothers-in-law.

Remember, whatever gets into the psyche, no matter how young, grows bigger with the years, and more powerful until growth is done.

Parents often strive, and successfully, to break up marriages they deem too early, or with one they think is the wrong one.

Do you want a heart-rending story? Some years ago a sick call came. I answered it. An elderly mother said, "Sit down. I want to talk to you before I make my confession. The doctor said I have cancer and I am going to die. [It smelled like it.] You know," she said, " I have been married forty-five years. I have five boys and one girl. Father, you got some of my boys out of jail several times, and I want to thank you. As you know, my husband is not a Catholic. Well, the Catholic man or the boy I was in love with when I was young my parents broke it up. This man I never loved, but I lived with him all these years. Now I'm going to die, and I thought you should know all of this."

I gave her the sacraments, took her to the hospital and later buried her, all with a heavy heart for her and for the poor kids whose parents allow them to have beaus or steady dates too early. That's what comes of this beau stuff with little ones.

A doctor does not need to have appendicitis in order to remove an appendix. Neither does a priest need to be married to know the psychology of it all.

My shoulders are wet from married people crying on them off and on, mostly on, over the years. So please give your love to your parents and to Jesus until you are old enough to get married. And parents, please give love and affection to your children through high-school years. I mean, manifest it.

Give people of other faiths a break. Do not force them to become Catholics. You can find out where they stand on the religion question the first time you are together.

If one religion is as good as another to them, then okay. It presents no great problem to become a Catholic. But if they are staunch in their own raising and conscience, please do not make it hard for them and for you, too, by being split on the religion question. You'll have a wall between you all your life-time. That's not fun, baby. That's what these people tell me. Of course, they won't tell anyone else.

I don't know how many times Protestants who were married to Catholics came to me and said, "Father, why don't you get up in that pulpit and tell your Catholic people not to marry us Protestants. It just does not work." You see, a Protestant is a Christian; a non-Catholic can be anything.

There are lots of problems to come up that no one thinks about beforehand. The Church knows it. She prohibits mixed marriages, but even the Church cannot forbid them. All have the God-given right to marry freely whom they will so long as God's rights and those of the children are safeguarded.

Often it is not so much a case of conscience as it is a case of ethnic hardheadedness. Some nationalities appear to be more stubborn than others, if I am allowed to tell it like it is.

This reminds me of a cute story. Three men were found guilty of a certain crime. The judge, trying to show compassion, said, "I allow you to select the kind of tree on which you must die from hanging." One said, "Hang me on a mighty oak." Another said, "Hang me on a shady maple tree." Pat said, "Hang me on a gooseberry bush."

It really takes a sense of humor to go through this life. A sense of humor means to see God in all things, as God wants us to see Him.

Tom. Have you ever done any religious work around a prison?

Fr. Yes, when I was at Catholic University forty years ago or longer, the St. Vincent de Paul Society couldn't find any volunteer to say Mass for the prisoners on Sunday for whom they rendered a service. I, all the way from Indiana, volunteered as a labor of love. These De Paul members hauled me out to the prison and back.

Before Mass I heard confessions. Most of the inmates were black. I suppose because D.C. was over half black too. In my book blacks are not as bad as whites. You know, I used to sit there hearing confessions and cry. Those dear men were better than I was, despite the fact they were prison inmates.

One of them told me a cute story. He put in a long-distance phone call to his mother in Schenectady, New York. The operator asked how to spell it. He said, "If I knew how, I would write her a letter instead of telephoning."

Joe. What's the oldest person you ever took into the Church?

Fr. An old soldier who said he was 106. His old son hated me for it, but I had to do God's work. It was his life. My duty was to bear witness, to get involved: to help him identify with Christ.

I like to tell this story on a man ninety-five years old. He had been away from the sacraments, for the want of a church close by, for about eighty years. He was afraid to come back after so long a time. One day it was awful hot as we went riding. I asked him all kinds of questions in relation to his life and the Ten Commandments. He answered them all by a yes or a no and often without any hesitation. Finally, down the road I spotted a huge tree alongside of the road. I said, "Let's stop in the shade for a while." He was agreeable. I said, "How about going to confession? We are here all alone." "I'm afraid," he said. "There is nothing to be afraid of," I said. "You just confessed everything you ever did, so now all you have to do is to say: 'Father, I want to make all that a matter for this good confession' and I'll give you absolution. You won't have to repeat it." He was pleased. The devil takes fear away in order to get us to commit sin; then, when we go to confession, he puts fear back.

Mary. What is bearing witness to or for Christ?

Fr. My bishop assigned me to a different parish. To build up to a little good will I used to go to a different filling station every time so as to get acquainted. This was an approach for bearing that witness you asked about and which Jesus commands.

One day the most popular young man in town came out to wait on me. He said, as he took my money, "I'd like to become a Catholic. What do I have to do?" I said, "You must take a course of instructions so as to know what it is all about. We don't force anyone. You must freely know what you are doing, then ask for it and live up to it."

He said, "I work here about seventeen hours a day, seven days a week. But if and when I find time, I'll let you know." That was it. He never found time.

Months later I took to bed with a bad case of influenza. A K.K.K. who had become a recent pal of mine called to visit me when he heard I was sick in bed. He informed me that Joe had leukemia and was going to die. So I got out of my sickbed and went at once to see Joe. A nice little woman came to the door when I knocked. She asked me what I wanted. I said, "Is this where Joe lives?" She said, "Yes." With that Joe recognized my voice and said, "Come in, Father." Joe was lying on a cheap cot in the center of the other room. He could hardly whisper, so weak was he.

Sizing up the situation, I said, "You better go to the hospital." He whispered, "I can't afford it." I said, "Go at my expense."

Next day when making the rounds in the hospital, to my surprise here was Joe in a five-bed ward. He said, "Here I am. I took you at your own word." I said, "I'm unhappy. As sick as you are, you should have a private room." He was moved to a private room.

I asked Joe if there was anything I could do for him. He said, "Yes, but I'm afraid. Did you ever break a plate-glass window downtown and be afraid to go home and tell your father?"

"I've got you," said I, as I quickly retorted. "You just told me you are going to die real soon. Are you afraid to meet your Heavenly Father and tell Him you broke a plate-glass window down on earth by not doing what is right?" He answered, "I've got you. Shine me up."

I realized the false propaganda that was being circulated at large, namely, "You go to that Catholic hospital and when you are half conscious, the priest will steal you and make you a Catholic." So I knew there was going to be blood on the moon because of this. But one who bears witness to and for Christ is thrilled no end at such. It's real fun.

However, I suggested to Joe that he had better tell his wife of his intentions, just in case. I put in a phone call to her. She appeared in five minutes. Waiting in the corridor for her, I said, upon her arrival, "Your husband wants to see you. I will wait out here to give you privacy." In a couple of minutes I rapped on the door and walked in.

As I did Joe was in a strong whisper: "Honey, meet our new pastor." That was a commitment after a fashion, or a mild profession of faith. He then proceeded to inform his wife that he wanted to become a Catholic and to do whatever that called for.

I told them that if he had never been baptized, Baptism was in order. If he had been, then confession was in order, followed by Communion and the Last Anointing. Then he asked for confession, saying to his wife, "Would you please step out of the room while I make my confession."

He was so weak, not mentally but physically, that when I heard his confession, I said to him, "I'll ask you questions on the commandments. For yes, squeeze my hand once; if lots of times, squeeze it lots of times. If the answer is no, then squeeze my hand twice." So I held a man's hand, and a man held mine. It was thrilling to prepare someone for heaven, one who was to go there so soon. The next day Joe died.

I did have sufficient presence of mind to ask him where and by whom he wished to be buried. I knew there would be trouble because of all this.

Joe's father was a kind of one-horse preacher, as the folk in town called him. He ran a grocery store. Maybe he knew his groceries, but not his Bible. However, he quit the church in which he grew up and in which he was baptized for a larger one, seemingly desiring to be a little duck in a big puddle. If he couldn't be the biggest one in town, he forsook the second one for the newest breed of the time, a very small church. This was the newest sect in the United States then. He preached now and then but mostly ran the show. He was now the biggest duck in the smallest puddle.

Having anticipated a peck of trouble over Joe's doing, to which I was an accomplice, I expected loads of trouble from the father. He called on me. He was emphatic that his boy should never be buried from the Catholic church. I got Joe to so state in the presence of his K.K.K. wife. She remained loyal to her husband despite her disappointment on that score.

The father said, "I'll not come to the funeral if it is held in the Catholic church." To this I responded, "That's your business. This is my business or duty."

Finally, I put the pressure on, by saying, "Listen, Reverend, if I a catholic priest were sick and sent for you on my deathbed, you would come, wouldn't you?" "Yes, sir," came the firm reply. And if I said, "Mr. Preacher, I, a Catholic priest, wish to join your church. You would accept me, not?" "Yes, sir," again came the curt reply. "And if I said, 'I want you to bury me from your church,' you'd oblige a dying man's last wish, not?" "Yes, sir," he said without the slightest hesitation.

At this point I said, "Reverend, what you would do for me, a Catholic priest, if I so requested it, is precisely what I am going to do for your son, even if not a living soul attends the funeral save for his wife and myself." The church was packed with Protestants and non-Catholics. Yes, the father was in the first pew.

Such are some of the thrills that come in a loyal, living priest's life. Jesus told His priests (the Apostles), "They have persecuted me; they will persecute you."

When speaking of witnessing for the Lord, another filling-station episode comes into the picture.

One morning, rather early, perhaps six-thirty, I drove into a station. No one came to wait on me. Time passed on. Still no attendant was on the scene. A horn toot or two died on the crisp morning air. At this point I crawled out of the car and lo, no one was in the cracker-box-like station.

Finally a youngish man was discovered squatting down in the sun on the warm side of the "box." Without the least semblance of any sign of rendering any service, he began to chew the priest out in terminology that was not exactly fitting for a prayer, albeit some of the same words are used in prayers.

As he remained squatting, with cross eyes he looked up at my face six feet two inches above the ground and said, "I never saw you before, but I suppose you are the local priest. I suppose you want some gas." "Please, sir," said I.

"Do you think you are going to get any? So you can forgive sins, eh?" he continued.

At that I gave him both barrels: "Not only can I forgive sins, but what is more, you have plenty of sins that need to be forgiven! I have stood here long enough to size you up. From the tip of your toes to the top of your head there is every indication that you are full of sin. Now, get up and get me some gas." At that he rose and got me gas.

Our Lord at times does seem to use muscular psychology. Here is another one for Ripley. That day was not over until that same young man was knocking at my door, saying "I want to go to confession to have my sins forgiven."

He was informed that he would have to study our Lord's religion, accept it freely; then he might go to confession, after he knew and understood what he was doing. He did come for instructions. There were two dogmas of the creed to which he objected most at the first. One was the forgiveness of sins, or confession, by the priest. The other was papal infallibility.

When the course of instructions were completed, the articles of the creed to which he objected most in the beginning, he came to like the best in the end: confession and papal infallibility. He was willing to become a Catholic, but he never came into the Church at that time. He did forty years later. His parents told him if he did they would commit suicide. That scared him out. He did not heed Jesus' words

(Matt. 10:42 ff.). Such was the interpretation put on freedom by those who yell most about Catholics having no liberty.

His wife and children all came into the church at that time, leaving this man to emulate the Emperor Constantine, who waited until near his death for so doing, so as to have baptismal innocence.

7

Marge. Tell us again about your first and last lie.

Fr. When I was a little nine-year-old boy, my mother gave me a store packet of wax beans to plant. She told me how and where to plant them. "Get the hoe hanging on the garden gate. Dig holes so deep [she hand-measured them], put two or three seeds in a hole. Cover over with about an inch of dirt. Plant them inside the gate in rows." This was sixty-six years ago, and I still remember it.

Well, inside the gate the ground was hard as a street pavement. I decided to spare my hands, which were now getting blisters. The thought struck me. Why not put a handful of seed in each hole? That will lessen or shorten the work.

Of course, I was done in no time. Mamma said upon my return, "Are you finished already?" "Yes," came the response. "You sure you put only two or three seeds in a hill?" "Yes," came the lie.

In a day or two the beans were up and growing. Each hill was as thick with new plants as the hair on a dog's back, a dead giveaway. I was caught in the act of having told a lie.

I learned then and there, always do and speak the truth and you won't have to remember what you do or say. Honesty is the best policy if you live long enough.

Pat. So you really spilled the beans.

Greg. Did you always insist that everyone become a Catholic?

Fr. No, not unless they so desired it. Four out of every hundred patients in the hospital were Protestant. When they came to die, if they asked for Baptism, I gave them that sacrament. Otherwise, I prayed with them or they prayed after me.

One time I was saying it and I used these words: "I am sorry for all the sins of my whole life, dear God; and I promise never to sin again." At that the sick Protestant said, "I won't say that, because I know I will sin again." At once I said, "I stand corrected," and continued, "Dear God, I promise I want never to sin again." To these words he said, "I'll say that." He had more sense than the priest.

I never prayed over them. I always asked them to repeat the words after me. These prayers embraced the act of faith, hope and charity, and contrition.

Debbie. Do you think your attitude towards that filling-station man was highly diplomatic?

Fr. Perhaps not in some people's way of doing things. But, you know, I never thought too much of diplomacy other than telling it like it is, for the simple reason it reminds me of the diplomat who said, "Guess how many fish I got in this bag and I'll give you both of them." Diplomacy smells, and not of fish either.

Frank. Which is the greatest of the virtues?

Fr. St. Paul speaks of faith, hope and charity. But the greatest of these is charity (I Cor. 13:1 ff.).

When speaking of diplomacy, I always think of the words of Isaias that St. Paul quotes: "I will destroy the wisdom of the wise, and the prudence of the prudent I will reject (I Cor. 1:19). St. Paul was no great diplomat as we understand the word today.

Paul also said in equivalent words that Christ sent him to

give testimony of the Word of God, "not with wisdom of words, lest the cross of Christ be made void" (I Cor. 1:17).

Prudence on the supernatural level is little more than charity or love. People can tell if you love and if you are sincere. They seem to sense it. You know, I averaged thirteen converts a year for forty years, whereas the national figures were about two per priest a year.

Tom. Will Jews get to heaven?

Fr. I hope so. They believe in God. And no one loves as the Jews love each other.

One day a priest went to the dentist. After completing his work, the dentist said, "No charge. You are a professional man, so my services are free to you."

The next day the priest sent a letter with some token gift of appreciation to the dentist.

In the course of a few days a minister had his teeth cared for. The dentist repeated his speech about free professional service. So the minister sent some literature in appreciation.

Finally a rabbi went to the dentist for professional service. The rabbi was accorded the same privilege. The next day the rabbi appeared with another rabbi. Such is their mutual love; the kind our Lord advocated, for He too was a Jew and said, "Love one another as I have loved you."

Speaking of Jews, one day I was riding on the train. A son of Abraham suddenly appeared and asked me if he might occupy the spare seat next to me. Of course, I consented, because I love everybody. Jews I like especially. They are smart. To repeat, our Lord was Jewish and His Blessed Mother was a Jewess. We don't disown them.

As we chatted my riding partner was speaking of anti-Semitism and anti-Catholicism. He spoke of a Gentile whom he had met up with and who was anti-Semitic. He said, "The village that I came from has not a Jew in it." "And what do you say when people belittle the Catholics?" I asked.

"I tell them that masterpieces are always in the minority."
You asked if Jews will get to heaven. I must answer the same
way Jesus answered. He said, "The Son of Man is not come to
judge." You know, even when Judas betrayed our Lord and
afterwards committed suicide, Jesus said, "He went to his
own proper place." What that place is, I don't know and shall
not presume to say. And no one has ever told us.

St. Paul says one of the signs of the end of the world
will be the conversion of the Jews to Christianity, while the
Gentiles (all others) will fall away. Read Romans for a head-
ache on this subject. We dare not be anti-Semitic; as Pius XI
said, "I think the Jews are God's pets. When the time comes
for the Jews to become Christian, watch them put the Catholic
Church over. They get things done."

Sometimes I think the greatest mistake most all people
make is to be careless with the way they use words. One
time a man was preoccupied as he sat in a hotel eating place.
The waiter approached and asked, "May I help you, sir?"
The guest said quite abruptly, "Do you have frog's legs?"
"No, sir," came the reply, "it is rheumatism that makes me
walk this way."

While speaking of diplomacy and tact, together with the
last crack I am reminded of this episode.

It was my policy to so frame my sentences or thoughts so
as to give no offense. Accordingly, whenever I was about to
go on my annual fishing trip I would remind the people, if
they had any pressing business to call the rectory before the
date of my leaving. Then at the last minute before departure
I would wish them well. Rather than say I hope no one dies,
etc., while I am gone, I would say, "I hope no one falls in
the cistern while I am gone." Such was hardly to be a happen-
stance.

One day the doorbell rang. As I opened the door there
stood Joe. I said, "Come in, have a seat." Joe was puffing.

Was it from climbing the many steps to the rectory, or was Joe disturbed? thought I. It did not take long to find out which.

Joe said, "Father, just because I fell in the cistern when I was a little boy you don't have to rub it in by referring to it all the time." With the proper apologies due to this lack of knowledge on my part, Joe left in a placated mood.

Joe. Does one have to join a labor union?

Fr. There are things only that one has to do sooner or later: obey the Ten Commandments, pay one's taxes and later on die.

Sometimes it may be to one's betterment to belong to a labor union and sometimes not.

One would think if the United States government was truly functioning in every detail and if the Church was functioning or reaching all people as Jesus intended, we would be in need of naught else besides.

Jesus said, "Render to Caesar the things that are Caesar's and to God the things that are God's." That sums up things pretty well.

It separates Church from state but does not separate religion from being practiced by the state or taken over by the state. When Jesus so spoke, He was admitting the existence of what we call temporalities. He also involved spiritualities. At the same time as He spoke, He put his O.K. upon morality, which is the way He wants us to act.

This means that the state is not to decide moral actions or releases therefrom, such as divorce, birth control, abortion, soldiering on the job, etc. The state was never sent to teach, but to practice whatever Jesus enjoins through His teaching Church; and to allow complete liberty and protection for the Church's ministry or mission.

However, since we confuse physical (or functional) liberty with moral liberty in the U.S.A., we are bound to be in a state of confusion all the time with religion getting the hind most. In fact, the U.S.A. was born of physical liberty.

The biggest union today is the A.F.L.–C.I.O. The former letters stand for American Federation of Labor.

What C.I.O. stands for, one cannot be too sure. It came into prominence back in the early thirties via Russian visitors or sojourners. Three brothers and not the bewhiskered brothers (cough drop) fame who left their razors at home. A news reporter in Chicago tried for weeks to find out what C.I.O. stood for but to no avail. This was after the 1929 stock-market crash and at the beginning of the depression. After quite some time the reporter wrote that "C.I.O." was to stand for "Committee on Industrial Organization." At that time the C.I.O. movement was antagonistic of the A.F.L.

"They" (I always wonder who "they" are) were striving to organize the laborers in my parish and of course all others.

One day Joe, a fine Catholic, and his fine non-Catholic friend came to my house to ask advice: "Should we or should we not join the C.I.O.?" My answer: "I would wait a while. Since the house of labor A.F.L. and C.I.O. cannot set its own house in order it would seem prudent to wait until they do. "What," I asked, "does the big wheel of the C.I.O. labor advise?" This is what he said, "The laboring man? We are not interested in the laboring man. We are only interested in making So-and-So President of the United States." "Will the both of you swear to that?" said I. "We are willing to swear, and so did sign a paper to that effect."

At the time, C.I.O. seemed to me to be the call letters for Communist International Organization, and it still so smells. Communism seems to be a front for Satan, it is so heavy with envy and prevarication.

It may not be diplomatic to so write, but the latest American fad is to tell it like it is. It's about time we got some gumption and had the honor of our convictions.

Even the little girl so expressed herself when some were asking why Apollo 14? She said, "So they can take the rocks back they took the last time from the moon."

The jewelry stores are filled with Communist emblems, such as the crowfoot and Churchill's victory salute. Many ears hear many different versions, as illustrated in the following account.

One time four bachelor girls were riding the train behind a well-dressed couple. One of the bachelors said, "Those people must have been at a musical last night because I heard her speak about a trained ear." The second said, "No, I thought they were at the zoo, they were speaking about the reindeer." The third said, "You are both wrong. I'm sure they are getting off at the next stop cause I heard her say, distinctly, 'Find out about the train, dear'." The fourth said, "I heard her make mention of the fact that it rained here." Finally one said, "I'll ask 'em what she really said." This was the reply, "I merely remarked to my husband, 'It rained, dear.' "

Debbie. The other Sunday I heard you read in one of the lessons from St. Paul, "to speak truth." Does one always have to tell all he knows?

Fr. Quite the contrary. There is not a person alive to whom we must tell all we know, not even to our father confessor, if it is not his business to know. What St. Paul is writing about is not to tell a lie. Paul was way ahead of us.

Today we hear people say, "Accentuate the positive." That is what Paul is doing in those words.

If we are going to speak, we should measure our words and speak what is on our speaking mind. But we never have to tell all that is in our mind, unless it is the other person's business to know.

Might the above paragraph be put in one sentence: "You can't hunt rabbits with a brass band." After all, everyone is entitled to the right of personal privacy. That is one reason for loving our Blessed Mother. She never told everything she knew. She kept the virtue of silence, which is so precious. The Bible says "she pondered all these things in her heart."

Every time one speaks a sentence, he opens up a little peephole in the mind. Present-day diplomacy contrives how to say something and at the same time keep those peep-holes plugged up. It is most disconcerting.

8

Marge. How come there is so much opposition to the Catholic Church?

Fr. You should know that the biggest clubs are always found under the best apple tree. You might as well ask how come Jesus was put to death. Ever hear of envy?

It was because Jesus opposed the physical freedom of the people and tried to get mankind to practice God's moral freedom. It won't hurt to repeat it here. Moral freedom is the liberty to act the way God wants us to act. Otherwise we always might enjoy physical freedom. For example: Do you think God cares whether a man parts his hair on the right or left side or even in the middle, unless such has to do with keeping his fastidious wife happy?

As was said before, physical freedom leaves one free to do what one pleases right or wrong. If you ask me, that's the fruit of the tree of good and evil whose fruit Mr. and Mrs. Adam ate up. It is the uppermost boast of all.

Moral freedom which allows only what is right or what we ought to do so as to please God—too often one finds few people to eat it up; hence is it that "the just man lives by faith," as St. Paul records.

We should never back away from moral liberty, because this liberty is founded on God, who is supreme truth. To say it again, "the truth shall make you free," said Jesus.

Mary. What's the toughest question ever put to you?

Fr. It came from my own mother. Time was when she came to be anointed and prepared for possible death and her son, the priest, did it—if not for sufficient illness (heart trouble), then because of sufficient age (83).

After administering the sacrament of the Last Anointing, Mother said: "I'm afraid to die." The language was not too clear, so I said, "What do you mean?"

Quick as a flash she replied, "Oh, I don't mean that I'm afraid of not going to heaven when I die. What I mean is, I'm afraid I might choke to death."

Having been disabused of any such likelihood, she said, "You priests know all the answers. How will I meet our Lord when I die?"

That sure was a toughie. Right now I said a quickie, "Come, Holy Spirit," and the needed answer came: "Mamma, you were always close to and a great lover of the Blessed Mother and Her rosary. She'll be there to present you to the Lord, Her Son." That pleased her.

Wouldn't you say those should ever be precious memories for her priest son!

Steve. The Bible says Jesus never went to school.

Fr. Let's look up the exact wording of the Bible. "How does this man come by learning since He has not studied?" (John 7:15). Don't you suppose that when God created Jesus' human nature, He gave Him all kinds of infused knowledge, and the same for His Blessed Mother!

Who could possibly have been a better teacher for Jesus the Son of God who is God. As the Son of God who is God, He knew and knows all things. However, as a human being but not a human person, the Bible says, He was *full* of wisdom (Luke 1:80; 2:40). Is this to say He had infused knowledge? I should think so. Adam had it; to what extent we do not know. Why wouldn't Jesus have had it to the fullest extent? The record says He was "full of wisdom," as we saw above. Besides, Jesus said "My teaching is not my own, but his who sent me" (John 7:16).

Do you know that one of the most important things in life is to read the Bible accurately and to have a big dictionary close by all the while so as to learn the precise meaning of words?

For example: A certain John was a professor of English at Boston University. He was a stickler for the correct and accurate use of words. One day John's wife, Mary, wished to go downtown. The streets were too icy to drive, so Mary boarded the streetcar that passes by the corner. She didn't discover it until she was asked for the token or streetcar fare. She had forgotten her pocketbook.

In a hurry, with no pocketbook containing the house key, Mary went in the back way. As she entered she found her husband spooning with the maid, and Mary exclaimed, "Why, John, I'm surprised."

John retorted, "No, Mary, I am surprised; you are amazed."

One time friend wife was doing a crossword puzzle. She got stuck and said to her husband, "What's the word for a female sheep?" Replied he, "Ewe, dear." And the fight was on.

Judy. How come you give boys the name Mary when you baptize?

Fr. Here are at least two good reasons. 1. The law of the Church prescribes that at Baptism a Christian saint's name be given.

Many people want their babies named after Grandpa or

Grandma. In such a case it might not be the name of a saint but rather the name of a Pullman car, or some new washing machine. To avoid hurt feelings I simply add on the name of Mary to whatever other name a boy or girl may be given.

2. After all, at Baptism everyone becomes Mary's adopted child; why not be named after Her for a good start in life? You'll never go wrong if named after Mary, and if you always say Her rosary she asked for.

Gus. But why give a boy the name of a woman?

Fr. Why not? Jesus' last name was Mary: "Is this not the son of Mary?" (Mark 6:3); "Is not His mother called Mary?" (Matt. 13:55).

One day a little boy started to school for the first time. The teacher asked him his name. He answered John Patrick Maria Toktry. The teacher said, "Whoever heard of a boy with a girl's name?" John Patrick Maria answered, "My mother in heaven is our Blessed Mother and I'm proud to be named after her. Mary is Her name. Mary is my name."

John Patrick Maria didn't do well in school after that ribbing. Neither did the teacher.

You know, if you get in bad with the kiddies you might just as well leave town.

Robert. Why do so many priests leave the priesthood today?

Fr. I don't know; I never asked them. But I did learn of one years ago who, after his first Mass celebration was over, said the following to his parents: "I have done what you wanted me to do. So now I am going to do what I always wanted to do. I am leaving today for New York to become a doctor."

Richard. Why did you become a priest, Father?

Fr. Because I always thought that was what God wanted me to do. I became a priest to give myself to help people and not to receive, and especially not to make money. Almighty God was preferred to the almighty dollar. As was said before, genuine love wants to give, wants to suffer as it gives.

Susan. What's the greatest thrill you ever had in the priesthood?

Fr. Teaching Protestants and others how little they know about our Lord's religion; then, to see them blossom out afterwards.

You won't believe this, but actually when I had taken people into the Catholic Church after a course of instructions and after they had received the sacraments, their own friends and relations would not recognize them. That's how much the grace of God would shine in them.

The same for fallen Catholics who returned to the sacraments. One time I "shined" a hospitalized woman up with confession, communion, and the Holy Anointing while her sister was gone for dinner, but at that sister's request.

When the sister returned after dinner and entered the sickroom where the patient was in the hospital, Mickey backed out, saying "Excuse me." Mickey did not recognize her own sister, there was such a marked change in her appearance after receiving the sacraments.

As a matter of fact, Mickey went down the corridor to ask where her sister was, and what had happened to sister during the dinner absence. Finally Mickey was directed back to the same Room 114 where the patient had been all the time.

I'll never forget it. The patient was married badly. In order to test her I said, "Your unlawful husband is willing to live with you as brother and sister for the sake of the children." She said, "I am, but I know he won't. So I won't promise." I said this to test her sincerity.

When I told her she was going to die, she said, "O.K., shine me up. There won't be any problem in that case."

Our Lady's Angelus was sounding at noon; in Her honor, at that precise moment I laid the consecrated host upon that dying woman's tongue. She died soon. Was that ever a thrill!

Really, it would be hard to say what ever gave me the biggest thrill. Each day is thrilling because the priest in his own person represents our dear Lord as well as all the people, both of whom have their sacrifices offered up to God by the priest.

In the Mass the priest offers the sacrifice of Christ on the Cross to God the Father in Jesus' own name. This is so because Jesus is not visibly present to do it. Jesus once visibly did it, as St. Paul says. But now He does it again and again till the end of time through His priests as the prophet Malachia says, "from the rising of the sun to its going down, my name is great among the Gentiles and there is offered in every place a clean oblation in my name."

Then too the priest in his own person takes all the little and big sacrifices of the people and unites them with Jesus' sacrifice in the Mass so as to make them pleasing and acceptable to God the Father.

As already stated, there is a terrific thrill in teaching converts. I don't like that word "convert." Non-Catholics or Protestants or what not do not as a rule have to "turn to God" to be Catholics. That's what the word convert means. It seems to me that good people, instead of turning, merely have to graduate from kindergarten to something higher than what little they now have or know. At least that is what they all say after coming into the Church.

There is so much bigotry in the world because of false propaganda and also because of bad example from Catholics.

When these dear souls find out it is entirely different from what they had been told, they become ashamed for allowing themselves to have become deceived.

Joe. Sometimes they backslide.

Fr. Yes, but when they come to die they always send for the priest. What does that prove?

There is one thing that always bothers me. Time and time again Protestants have said to me, "The best person I ever knew was a Catholic," but it never occurs to them that it is the Catholic religion that makes them so good. This is referring to the Sacraments and the rosary.

You know what? I've always said if I believed only half of the false propaganda against the Catholic Church that Protestants believe, I'd hate the Church too.

Or, to turn it around, if Protestants knew half as much about our Lord's religion as I do, they'd be twice as good Catholics as I am. How little they know! Yes, and how dumb and superstitious they think we are!

It would be interesting for only one to be present at a course of instructions. To begin with, I ask two questions of any and all. Most always I get the same answers, which are wrong.

1. When you and I were born into the world, were we children of God? Invariably the answer comes, "Yes, indeed."

2. Did Jesus Christ exist before He became the baby Jesus in His mother's womb? Invariably the answer comes, "No."

Is Jesus God? *"No," would come the answer.* "He is God's Son, but He is not God and never existed till conceived by the Holy Spirit." This is also wrong.

Now comes the shocker. I ask them to take the Bible (usually a Protestant version) and read the answers to those first questions.

They have been taught that Catholics don't read the Bible and are not even allowed to have one in their possession. Producing a Bible, therefore, for them to read is the first shock. Next, please turn to John's Gospel, chapter 1:1 ff. When they don't know where to look for that, embarrassment sets in. Next, when they read, "But to as many as received him he gave the power of becoming sons of God; to those who believe in his name: who were born not of blood, nor of the will of the flesh, nor of the will of man, but of God," they see their mistake.

Next we turn to chapter 3 in John and find out how to become a child of God through rebirth in Baptism.

As to the other question—did Jesus have any existence before He became a baby?—we read, "The word was made flesh." "The word was God." If He is God, then we better pay attention to all that He says. We better believe all. To believe and try to do all means to be Catholic.

It is that simple. Those poor people think if they believe anything they do not understand, it is an insult to their own intelligence, whereas we say we love to believe what Jesus revealed and the Church believes and teaches especially when we do not understand it, such as the many mysteries starting with the Blessed Trinity, the Blessed Mother, the Blessed Sacrament, etc., etc., etc., and a thousand other mysteries.

In this way not only do we not insult our own intelligence but we do the greatest worship and honor to the intelligence of God, who reveals his mysteries. We thank Him for letting us in on His mysteries. Otherwise such professional truths would never occur to us.

I don't suppose this thought ever entered your mind: the greatest honor we can give our mother is to believe that we are her child. I've always claimed that instead of celebrating our birthday and claiming all the attention and honors on that day, by rights all the acclaim should go to our mother after God.

Let us return once again to the subject of corporal punishment. As stated above, I absolutely do not believe in it. It makes children mean. They simply bide the day when they can get even with their parents. This usually breaks out when the child becomes a teenager. It is not essentially identified with the teenage. Accidentally it is. This is to say the child has nursed certain hatred or grudges all these years until it is old enough, strong enough, to rebel so to get even. There is nothing, simply nothing, that a child hates and deplores more than to be accused falsely. This holds true especially if the matter regards sex.

Example: Many teenagers have said this to me: "My parents told me nothing. Now they take it for granted that I know everything. They have falsely accused me all along. I decided I had just as well do these things I am accused of and really be guilty."

They are old pros and seem to think their children are too. This teenage of rebellion has been in a stage of gestation for many years. Sometimes it starts at about the age of four, albeit birth of the rebellion does not occur until teenage time.

Then we ask, Why? Why not! What we sow in the psyche, the psyche must reap—only, with compound interest annually till teenage time.

If a child must be whipped, then let it happen before the child is four years complete. The age of four is set because very few children ever remember for life anything that occurs before that age. And who would want a child to remember forever that he had a licking in place of love? It is sufficient for corrective purposes if the child remembers it for a month or two (if it does) so as to remedy its faults.

The unfortunate thing is this: most parents lick their kids mostly when they blow a fuse. And the child knows it. Such correction is wasted effort and highly detrimental to a child. This is perhaps the most potent reason why children should never be licked after the age of four. They should have no such memory of a loving parent's becoming unduly angry.

It was stated above that what we sow in the psyche must

be reaped by the psyche. It would be better to say what is put in the psyche of a child grows therein. I like to use this example to illustrate:

When I was five years old, the family sent me to school one June 5 in order to get me out of the house during the birth of a new sister. When I came home from school, I found my mother in bed and the infant lying on a pillow in the corner. My father hurried me out to the garden to help him. I carried a butcher knife for some reason. In my excitement, which lingered on, I wanted to know where that baby had come from and so I slashed the index finger to the bone. It left a scar after healing. The scar grew apace with the years. So much did it grow that at maturity the scar itself was as long as the finger at the time it was cut. The same holds true with what goes with the psyche in early childhood. It grows stronger and stronger until too powerful to be controlled. It is in this that good children or bad children become good teenagers or bad teenagers.

To repeat, children whipped after the age of four will remember it all the rest of their lives. This everlasting memory will ride along on an ill will. What chance love!

Parents don't realize it, but when they pick up a crying child and start patting it on its bottom, this, while having the soothing effect of stopping the crying, at the same time is playing a soothing tune on the erotic centers located in that region.

True, the Bible reads, spare the rod and spoil the child. At the same time the Bible says, if one is obliged to whip, then "dress the child's sides." There are no erotic centers there.

The old saying still holds good: he rules best who rules least. Jesus spoke more about love in connection with His commandments. All punishment, according to Him, is reserved to the Father in the next life.

President Nixon reminds us that no one alive but has lived through war some time some place in this world. To this might well be added the further truth: it is hate that has congealed the emotions of countries to fight wars rather than let love jell them to live in peace. Satan wins again. This is not going Her way.

Few parents know the distinction between penal laws and moral laws. Penal laws bind under pain of penalty; moral laws bind under pain of sin.

If parents would list a number of things they demand under pain of penalty, they should at the same time list the penalty. But no corporal punishment. Then, if a child is intent on performing some act that is on the penalty list, he must understand that thereby he is asking for a penalty. He has no one to blame but himself.

For example, at the orphans' villa we had a list of penal rules for the usual offenses. The penalty may have been "no movie" or "no candy" or "no pie," etc.

Hence the child always knew in advance what the consequences would be for certain types of misbehavior. If the other children got to go to the show, the rest of us would say with a smile, as we were leaving for the show, "We're sorry you can't go along." This sort of rubbed it in, in a nice way, with good results.

Corporal punishment was never on the list with penal laws. My mother used to say, and she was tops on this after raising nine, the quickest way to a child's heart is through its stomach. I can add to this, the quickest way to a man's heart is through his wallet, whether he be friend, priest, or husband.

At the villa a lot of candy was always on display with no lock and key. The children were put on their own honor. They were taught that honor is more important than money. So they guarded the candy. I'm afraid more youngsters are ruined by fly swatters than by flies.

As a matter of fact, most offenses are perpetrated because of hate, the mother of envy. One makes a great mistake by ever losing one's temper when dealing with a child. In reality that very thing is uppermost in the child's mind, even though the child is too small to speak about it. Thinking requires no words. To ignore a child is always more effective than corporal punishment. Children want to be recognized. They crave attention. Their ego calls for food the same as their tummies. Let their ego starve for that recognition at stated periods; that will bring them around.

Mary Alice, a thirty-year-old woman, recalled to my mind an episode from her early life. She had been ugly to her mother some twenty-five years before in my presence; at five years of age she said to her mother, "I won't do it." "You happened to hear it," she recalled, after those many years, "so when I turned to you for some acknowledgment, you ignored me. You said, 'If you treat your mother that way, you are no friend of mine.' That nearly broke my heart. It did far more than a licking could have done. Instead of making me rebellious, as most lickings do, it made me remorseful. It has stayed with me all these years."

You know, that statement "I won't do it" always makes me think of Eve, who said to God equivalently, "I won't do it." The whole world has been paying for it ever since. Little wonder the Old Testament Scriptures advise "breaking the child's will."

Little wonder the only song that ever came from heaven had as its main theme "Peace on earth to men of good will."

There are many little tricks that get results. All grow out of love. One day a rap came at my door at the orphans' villa. It was Sister Superior informing me that two of the girls in about the sixth grade had run away. She said, "Since you are newly in charge, we'll let you start right off on this case. What shall we do?"

In response I said, "I will look after it, but please tell all others to say or do nothing. "But aren't you going to call the police?" she inquired. "No," said I. "The police will spot these jayhawking kids downtown, like chickens walking in the night, in a few minutes. They will return them here." In ten minutes the doorbell rang. There stood a cop with the two girls. As ordered to do, they were sent to my room, scared to death. A faint knock came, which they hopefully wished would not be heard. I said, "Come in," in a most pleasant voice, without ever turning to look in their direction. All of a sudden I was most busy writing at my desk. Still not looking up, I let them stand there, excusing myself in a most pleasant tone of voice. Then I said, "Please have a seat."

Finally I turned to them and said, "What can I do for you?" By this time they could detect from the tone of my voice that I was in no bad mood as most would expect under such circumstances from almost every superior. Sheepishly came this response, "Father, we ran away, and the police caught up with us and brought us back." "I don't believe any such thing, that you ran away. You are too nice to do a thing like that. Here's what you did. You are great friends. You were out on our grounds walking and talking, talking and walking, with locked arms. As you walked you talked. As you talked you walked. Before you realized it, you were downtown. The police picked you up because they noticed you acted like strangers in town."

Shortly after that the bishop transferred me elsewhere as a troubleshooter. However, now and then I did return to the villa for business. As usual the children gathered around me and hung on. Finally I excused myself so that I might be about my business. The youngsters all scattered save two. "Do you remember us, Father?" they said. "I'm sorry, but I don't." "We are the two girls who ran away, but you said we didn't." There never was any further trouble, because they succeeded in getting under no one's skin. They were not challenged to repeat their prank. Love took over. Stewing in their own fat while they waited was sufficient punishment. The surprise treatment was challenging to every fiber of their souls.

Bob. Our original question was never answered.

Pardon me for getting off the track. Since you ask what was the greatest thrill I ever had, perhaps you mean experience. I had this experience. I instructed the people in church that if they ever knew of a fallen or sick Catholic or any sick or interested Protestant, they should let me know.

One afternoon the phone rang. A voice said, "Come down to Tom's residence. He should be a Catholic. His elderly wife just used our phone to call the doctor. They have no phone, so she asked to use ours." I departed for the sick man's home immediately. I pulled up to the curb right behind the non-Catholic doctor. Being twenty years or so younger than the doctor, I beat him into the house. The wife and the bachelor daughter (about 35 years old) were standing on the front porch to receive the doctor but not the priest. They did not know I was coming. If it had not been for the doctor's presence, I doubt I would have gotten in. I started in first and found the sick man. The doctor was polite. He said, "Your services are more important than mine," so he waited till I got through. I gave the sick man Holy Communion after hearing his confession and anointing him, together with all the sacraments and prayers for the dying. I told him I would bring Communion again in the morning if he was still alive.

When I arrived the next morning, the wife said, "There's no use to go in to see him, because he doesn't know anybody or anything. [She was very bitter.] He does not recognize us. He doesn't speak." I said, "It wouldn't hurt to try. Sometimes God fixes things so the priest can do what others can't do."

I entered the room and closed the door. And behold, the sick man was very much conscious. He never stirred till I got the door shut. He only whispered; I had to stoop over so my ear was close to his mouth in order to hear.

He put his arms around me and hugged me and said, "I have prayed for over forty-five years for this, so I could die in peace. Lest my wife talk me out of it, I am playing possum and acting as if I don't know anything or anybody. Don't let on." Then I left. He died in a day or so of a broken heart, the post mortem showed. A doctor discovered it was dry blood in his heart that had killed him—blood turned to gravel.

9

Speaking about what a priest sometimes can do, I might tell you this story.

When I was chaplain of that hospital for five years, one day a banker was brought in. He had shot himself. They had him in the operating room. The surgeon was scrubbing up, as they call it, for the operation to remove the bullet from the man's head. The suicide was still on the ambulance cot on the floor as I entered.

The non-Catholic doctor—and Sunday-school teacher—said in a rather sarcastic tone of voice, out of his envy of the priest, "You can't talk to him. He's completely out." "It won't hurt to try," said I. "What is his first name? Sometimes the priest can do what a doctor like you cannot do." Kneeling down on the hard tile floor in the operating room, I put my mouth right over his forehead, not at his ear, and said slowly, "Gus, tell God you are sorry for this." Gus opened his eyes. He responded. Tears ran down both cheeks. I said again,

"Tell God you are sorry for this, and ask Him to take you to heaven."

This was a doctor who always ribbed the priest about religion. So one day I got him to admit that he did not believe in religion. He taught it, he admitted, solely to build up his practice. One day he asked for it, so I said to him, "If I didn't know any more about my religion than you do about your medicine, I'd have to pull in my shingle."

You know, speaking of my experience in the hospital, it still scares me when I think about it. I discovered that most non-Catholics know but very little about God, religion and dying. Some even ask the doctor to give them a shot so they won't know when they pass on in death. Is that not frightening? I want to die with my eyes open. Really, that should be the happiest moment of one's life, the moment one dies and goes to meet God and His Blessed Mother, rather than the old boy who is waiting to take people to the other place. We were created to have God as our guest in this life so we could be His guest in the next.

That last paragraph is in no wise to be taken as a slap at anyone. It is a gesture of love, to which commitment I have been dedicated for fifty years. No, God is not dead even though He walks this earth in the hearts only of His followers.

Linda. Does a priest get much consolation?

Fr. Some people build him up and some build him down. If one is going Her way and is really dedicated to Her Son, our Lord, then that one gets all the consolation needed through God's grace. With St. Paul I can say, I count it a joy to suffer for Christ. You have to learn to take it. It is a labor of love for the good Lord. Love loves to suffer. Children usually build the priest up, and the oldsters (25–65) build him down. There are some gems that are exceptions.

Our dear Lord said it all when He said "out of the mouths

of babes, etc." One day after church one Sunday a man was waiting for me. As I came out he said, "I want to shake your hand. That was the finest sermon today that I have ever heard."

The next day I got a letter from a woman who wrote "that was the worst sermon, Sunday, I ever heard." Of course, I thanked both of them. The good Lord has a way of keeping us humble or honest, never forget that. He also said on occasion, "If these keep silent, the stones will cry out" (Luke 19:40).

Speaking of sermons, I made a deal with the Blessed Mother and the Holy Spirit to always tell me what to say and I would say it as well as take the heat. They never failed me, and I got plenty of heat for it too.

What people say doesn't mean too much. One should never take people too seriously and above all, one must never take one's self too seriously. God is the judge.

One of my charges once was a place that had asked the bishop to remove the pastor. One Sunday I reminded them of this fact. I also reminded them, if and when they desired my removal, not to go to the bishop but to come to me and I would go to the bishop for them. I also said, "I think we will have a glorious future. Our Lord said unless the grain of wheat dies it will not bring forth new fruit. Your parish has been dead a long time: now is the time for it to grow new fruit."

One day I was gunning for new prospects, either Catholic or Non-Catholic. It made no difference. I stopped at the home of a couple old enough to be my parents and asked them if they knew of any prospects. They mentioned one. I said, "I'll go there right now. Where do they live?" As they told me that they also said, "Don't go there. She will insult you." I said, "Now I have to go because I love to be insulted for our Lord's sake. (See Acts 7:24; Rom. 8:17; II Cor. 4:8-9; II

Thess. 1:5, 2:12; I Pet. 2:20, 3:14; Apoc. 2:10.) I departed to be insulted. As I came up on the front porch the devil almost had me scared to knock on the door. As I did the door came open and lo, there was the nicest, most polite woman I had ever met. She said, "How do you do, Father. Won't you come in? Take that good chair. Here, have a smoke. You know, I have been wanting to come and see you to take instructions in the faith." To make a long story short she became one of the best "converts" I ever had. Thus was Satan's envy defeated.

Pat. What's the biggest boner you ever pulled?

Fr. That's a dilly. It's on the top of my head there to remain forever. I'll never forgive myself for it.

One day when I was new in town, in the middle of the afternoon the phone rang. A woman's voice said, "Isn't it too bad about Mrs. Florence Jones"? I said, "What happened?" "Didn't you know she died?" came the reply. She hung up, and so did I. Immediately I got into my car and hurried down to the Joneses. Putting on a sort of somber, dignified appearance to meet anyone coming to the door, I knocked. Who do you think opened the door? It was Mrs. Florence Jones herself! She had a neighbor lady sitting in a high chair out in the kitchen and was giving the woman a hairdo.

What bugs me is not the mistaken information that came over the phone but that I had stupidly failed in my hurry to find out who was calling. One should always know to whom one is speaking on the phone before he ever receives or imparts a message. I still could kick myself at that boneheaded mistake. It has stunned me for well over thirty years.

This was the place the bishop had sent me to as a troubleshooter. The men were dragging their feet about monthly Holy Communion. Finally one Sunday I had the uncontrollable impulse to make this outrageous statement. "You better live in the state of grace. Six months from now we will have a tragedy in the parish."

Well, the week before the six months had expired, the sisters brought that whole statement of the past to my attention. They said, "We are counting the days until your predicted tragedy of about six months ago occurs. There are only seven days left. Next Sunday will be the last day."

As a matter of fact, I had to ask them what they were talking about. I had not thought of it since. The very thought had completely escaped me. It was Holy Name Communion Sunday. What do you suppose happened?

About 7 A.M., before the eight-o'clock Mass started. I was called to the home of one of the trustees. Out in the garage this man had hanged himself. There was no more dragging of feet after that.

A priest can expect to meet up with cranks almost anywhere and at any time. For a period of several weeks I received anonymous letters telling me to leave. I never breathed this to a soul. I even got a small vial of wine in mail using the same handwriting as in the letters. There were instructions packaged together with it; they read like this: "This is a sample of delicious Mass wine. Take all in one draught to get the greatest benefit and to appreciate its bouquet. We will call next week to take your order."

I never breathed it to a soul for the following reasons. (*a*) I always taught the kiddies if you want a secret kept, never tell a soul. Our Lord said, "Tell no man," but the more He told them not to tell the more they spread it around. (*b*) I figured if I told no one, then the sender sooner or later would be dying to find out if I had got the messages. It would set him a worrying, and worrying I was not doing, so let him worry, or fry in his own fat, thought I. Time disclosed someone was trying to find out, but I never pursued it and still do not know now or ever did. I did not want to know because of charity to all and malice to none.

Instead of sampling the wine as the instructions read, I mailed it to Loyola Medical School in Chicago for analysis. The analysis came back: "Mass wine charged with poison," the name of which I now fail to recall.

Anyway, this poison was intended to bring on a condition of diarrhea (dysentery) that no medicine could overcome, with the result being a gradual death from slow, constant, intermittent evacuation.

One day one of the trustees stopped me on the street. He said, "Father, I understand you have been receiving anonymous letters." I neither admitted it nor lied about it. Sure, as written above I had been getting them. They were always postmarked on Sunday at 4 P.M. in a neighboring city.

When the poisoned wine trick did not succeed, a letter came saying, "Be out of town by November 11th or you'll get a bullet in your heart."

This is one again for Ripley. November 11 is Armistice Day. Believe it or not, I was delivering the funeral eulogy for the wife of the aforementioned trustee as the whistles and bells were commemorating Armistice Day in said city at 11 A.M.

This is not to say that said man was in on it or that it was his thing. Someone could have sounded him out.

"Judge not," says our Lord. I do not know, and do not even suspect, that the trustee was involved. However, that was the end of the so-called threats. It was not yet the end of the Klu Klux Klan, as we shall see later on.

Every man in town, save one, belonged to the K.K.K. One of the ministers, pastor of the largest church in town, was chaplain of the Klan.

All K.K.K. officers' titles begin with a *K*. Example: The

chaplain was called the Klud; the sheriff or sargeant at arms, the Kligrapp; the council, the Konklilium.

I had at a later date access to D. C. Stephenson's "little black box" of state-wide newspaper fame. It contained the list of all members state-wide.

One Sunday morning, as I was hearing confessions before Mass as usual, there was a lull. It was in early August and hot. It being stuffy, as the box always is, especially in summer, I made for the front door to get a sniff of fresh air. As I was going down the front steps Joe and his wife were coming up the steps. They were from a neighboring town in my territory that had no Catholic church. Joe's wife stopped me. She said, "Father I have something for you." The middle-aged woman began riffling around in her purse as women usually have to do to find what they are looking for. Had it been Christmas time, I would not have wondered, but it being summer, I did wonder what was forthcoming.

Eventually the woman handed me a handbill. On it was this printed message: "Rev. DeLong will give the lowdown on the Catholic Church this P.M. at 2:00 in the town hall. All K.K.K. members please be present. I defy the Catholic priest to be present. Come on, show your stuff!"

In a corner in fine print were these words: "A silver offering will be taken."

After reading that, I had more of the sniffs than I was after, so distraught was I. Something seemed to start at my toes and come up to my mouth with an intense zip. I thanked the woman, but kept the notice.

I returned to the confessional box. I never will know whether I said, *Ego te absolvo"* or *"Ego te baptizo"* after that.

This all happened right before the last and 10 A.M. Mass. I was challenged to commit myself for the Lord. I must accept it to bear witness in His behalf. It was my duty, thought I, a young man.

The next thing was to find a couple of trustworthy laymen to be present to act in my defense (not as bodyguards) just in case a libel suit might follow in such a fracas.

Everyone I contacted begged off with the same excuse: "It is beneath your dignity to get involved in such an affair." I thought differently. Finally I thought of an Irishman who was a junk dealer. He had a big, strong son. He too begged off with the same excuse as the others, until I told him he was a coward. "Look, see what he says: 'I defy the priest to be present. Come and show your stuff.' " Does it say that?" he said. "Then we'll have to go." So go we did.

The father and his son were instructed on the way (8 miles) over to the town of the meeting just why I wanted two men. They were informed to keep away from me so as not to appear to have come with me. However, they were always to stay within hearing range—close enough to hear any and all that would be said by me or by them, if anything, that might cause a lawsuit.

We arrived at the town hall. The heat was terrific (from the sun), so much so that chairs had been carried out of doors under the shade trees. Men only were gathering. My two buddies remained in the car until the works started. We were parked alongside the curb on the opposite side of the street from the city hall, quite some distance away.

I got out and walked over through the big yard where the chairs were set up. There was a platform constructed of carpenter's horses with planks across their tops. Standing on this platform, about half the size of a boxing ring, were a few persons. I knew none of them. One of them was a woman who, I learned later, was the preacher's second or third wife.

As I approached I noticed this woman grab some man by the vest. With a look of despair on her face, she pointed to me as I walked in to the meeting grounds. When I saw that, I must have grown twice my size in strength. Those actions and looks of despair showed me at once that they were licked right then. It also indicated they never had expected the priest to be present as advertised. That was all a buildup for a sizable meeting and "silver collection."

Well, I walked over to the side of the town hall, away from the chairs and crowd. I sat down on the ground with my back against the building.

This was done as a means of self-protection. No one could approach from the rear and slug me, and if anyone aproached from either side of me, I would be able to see them coming by peripheral vision. In those days I could have licked Jess Willard.

The meeting opened on time per schedule, with about two hundred present. The minister announced that the meeting would open with that beautiful patriotic song "America," or, "My country, 'tis of thee."

"By the way" said he, "Catholics are not allowed to sing it. They don't know it. But once in a while one is stubborn or bullheaded and sings it anyway. Then when they come to that beautiful passage 'land of our pilgrims' pride, land where our fathers died,' they change the words to read, 'Land of the Popes and where the dagoes died.' "

With that as an introduction the woman began singing, "My country, 'tis of thee." Her key or pitch was just right for me. So I opened up on all twelve cylinders in order to give the lie to what he had said about our being forbidden to sing it, or that we did not know its words. Then I purposefully dragged it out, or slowed down the singing, so much so that when she was finished with the word "thee" in the first line, I was just singing the word " 'tis."

In that way I stole the whole show away from her. That made the preacher furious, and I paid for it during a verbal fusillade that lasted well over two hours.

The preacher showed courage, if courage is the word to

use when someone is being defamed. All the sinful, obscene, dirty words I had heard or read off and on in thirty years in restrooms just by chance or from some town alley rat the first years in school, the preacher used that day.

It ought to be said here that shortly before the singing, if I read lips correctly, the preacher and his wife were trying to find out the name of the priest as they all looked in my direction.

There was a priest by the name of Father Peters farther on down the road. It appeared they mentioned his name by way of identification, the way their lips moved. He was a shy, timid, saintly priest, the very opposite of myself.

The seat I took over against the wall was at right angles to the crowd and the speaker's stand. As the gentleman spoke I could keep my right eye on him and my left eye on the audience. Every now and then he would get off a crack that pleased the crowd. Then they thundered their applause. If it was a remark that I could concur in, I would clap my hands also and smile at the audience, whose eyes were then upon me; and I winked at them with my right eye as I turned my head back and forth, to the dismay of the preacher. That burned him up no end. He was not getting under my skin. Of course, when he used obscenities, as he did several times toward the end of his exhaustion, and the crowd cheered, I remained silent. I did not and could not participate in such.

For example, toward the end of his speech when he saw I was going to remain and answer his challenges, he made some obscene remarks about Daddy Peters, etc., and added further, "You are not my father. I won't call you Father. I'll call you Daddy." "Daddy Peters, etc., etc." were the obscenities.

The guy, with the help of the evil spirit, was clever, but not clever enough for one who had put his trust in the Holy Spirit (*Dabitur vobis inilla hora*) while going Her way.

During the course of his many, many outrageous sinful statements he laid himself wide open, as they say in boxing. This he said: "We have as a guest today a Catholic priest. I understand he has in his possession a little pamphlet put out by Bishop Noll, the Holy Roman Catholic Bishop Noll. I won't call him Bishop Noll, I'll call him Old Man Noll. In this pamphlet Old Man Noll has listed all the so-called ex-priests and ex-nuns of the country, and my name is the first one in the booklet. I'll tell you a good joke on that," he said. "When that pamphlet came out and I heard about it, I ordered a hundred copies. It sold for one dollar apiece. I signed my name to the order as Patrick Flanagan, and Old Man Noll thought I was an Irish Catholic, so he sent me the hundred for nothing. I beat old Man Noll out of $100."

Such was the nature of mob psychology with its envy and hatred.

With that detail the crowd applauded loudly, while I remained silent, of course. A gentleman is not allowed to applaud a thief.

The preacher laid himself wide open for a fierce thrust. After the applause the preacher proceeded to anticipate any remarks on my part. "In that little book Old Man Noll says I'm crazy. Maybe I am. I'm not denying it. In that book he says I beat up on my wife. So what? Just the other day my wife and I passed a Catholic priest and she spoke to him. I told her if she ever did that again I'd slap her d—— face." (With that the crowd cheered loudly.)

Finally, exhausted from the heat, anger, and effort, the preacher said, "Now I defy the priest to answer my charges." With that remark he sat down exhausted. I never had so many eyes upon me in such perversity.

In order to build up the audience for my remarks I remained seated on the ground for a few moments, which must have seemed an eternity to them. It may have appeared that I was scared, but I was in my glory.

Before referring to my remarks, in brief it should be said: I had been ill at ease about Bishop Noll's pamphlet. Indeed a DeLong was on the first page, but there was no photo. How would I know if this DeLong was the same DeLong? I just could get involved in a libel suit. The pamphlet stated that a certain DeLong was mentally underprivileged and had served time in three different institutions. It also stated that in a nearby town prior to this, the natives heard a woman's screams. Upon invesigation they found the preacher's wife, Mrs. DeLong, with her head hanging out the upstairs window, with her husband, the preacher, beating up on her.

Finally I rose and walked over before the crowd. I chose not to stand on the platform for fear of foul play—falling, that is. It was interesting. In those days the stiff sailor straw hat was in style. On the inside of my sailor straw I had a piece of paper upon which I had jotted a word or two of his many charges, together with the Holy Ghost's instant reply, to aid my memory. When I rose to speak, I was well fortified.

My speech opened like this, as I recall: "Fellow citizens of Black County, I am not Daddy Peters. I am Daddy Scheetz, chaplain over at the hospital. [With that statement a chorus of oh's and ah's went up.] If I mistake not I have seen some of you people either as patients or as visitors of some of the patients. The Reverend gentleman has asked me to answer his charges. So I will do. However, first we must establish common grounds on which to operate. You have demonstrated by your cheers here this afternoon that you are in full accord with the Reverend gentleman and out of accord with me, regardless of his obscenities.

"Normally, it would do no good to attempt to answer his charges with you people serving on the jury who are out of sympathy with me and in sympathy with the preacher. You are smart enough to know that. So am I. Ordinarily such would be the case. But today we are going to have an exception to such a situation. The Reverend gentleman who addressed you publicly admitted, here, this afternoon, that he is crazy. I am not crazy. Take a good look at the Reverend gentleman; then take a good look at me. Secondly, the Reverend gentleman told you with his own mouth, and you heard it and you applauded him for it, that he is a liar and a thief. He obtained books by fraud valued at $100. The Reverend gentleman admitted that he is a liar and a thief. I am not a liar and a thief. Are you going to believe him who says he is a liar and a thief in preference to one who is not a liar and a thief? Take a good look at him, then take a look at me." Things were getting too hot for the preacher, so he pulled out.

"The Reverend gentleman made some obscene remarks about priests and sisters," said I. "And you applauded him for it. Then you take your sick to that Catholic hospital where I am chaplain to be nursed by those same dear sisters whom he maligned today, along with your supporting applause.

"I would have you know I have two sisters that are nuns. I wish God would grant me the power of miracles so that I might transport them instantly as did Habacuc with Daniel, the one on one side of me and the other on the other side of me. I would then defy any one of you to produce a wife or a daughter half so pure and chaste and beautiful as either of them.

"Now, if any of you is a man, he will come up and punch me in the nose for such a remark. . . . I don't see anyone moving. You remind me of the words of Jesus to the Pharisees: "You hypocrites. Whited sepulchres full of dead men's bones. The poison of asps is under your tongues." On and on I went, till the charges were all answered.

To make a long story short, that broke the back of the K.K.K.'s in northeastern Indiana.

Every now and then I would meet up with someone who would say, "I never belonged to the K.K.K.'s." Whereupon my stock remark was, "Shame on you. Why, if my patriotism or 100 per cent Americanism had been challenged, at the small cost of ten dollars I would have signed up too. No one ever so challenged my patriotism."

With that remark they usually broke down, and admitted it, seeing that it did not bother me in the least whether they had or had not joined.

It was reported at the time that if any member were ever interrogated as to his membership, interrogation automatically discharged him. Then he would have to be sworn in again at the next meeting. That way they could swear they did not belong. I don't know if that was true or not.

One day a friend of mine who was a Mason asked what the Catholic Church had against the Masons. I explained that the French Revolution didn't leave a very good smell in the mind of the Church. Further, the Church has always claimed, and rightfully so, that the Church as well as the state, and even parents, have the right to know what any or all their children might be doing all the time. My friend agreed. He then went on to say, "Now I see why. The K.K.K.'s was spread by federal judges in the secret Masonic halls in Indiana. I'd give my right arm if I had never joined the K.K.K.'s. As to the Masons, I have never gone back to a meeting since the federal judge from Indianapolis in all his robes told us to join the K.K.K.'s. I thought my brother Mason, a federal judge, ought to have been worthy of trust.

There is something screwy someplace, it seems to me. It was alleged that Mr. Harding was not eligible for membership in Masonry because he had black blood in him. When he became President of the United States, to the surprise of all the honorary degrees of Masonry were conferred upon him and he accepted them. In that way Harding would know what was brewing, not as President but as a Mason.

When Vice-President Coolidge surprisingly became President at the death of the incumbent President, he refused the honorary degree. He was unloaded for the second full term. His secretary, now dead, said that's what killed him. He mourned himself to death over the misinterpretation of his since famous statement made in the Black Hills of Dakota, "I do not choose to run," in place of the inferred alternative, "I prefer to be drafted," which he thought the boys would take for granted. Too bad we have so many little governments within the United States government. Lincoln said that if the United States should ever fall, it would be from within.

As to Harding's untimely death, we have no proof. Silence in these times is therefore the better part of valor.

This should be stated here in deference to one man in the K.K.K. crowd. As soon as I began to pick the Klud's tail feathers by answering his charges, he tore out. One man ran over to him and was heard to curse him out and say, "You defied him to answer your charges. Stay and face it." But he moved along. About that time his wife yelled out, "The next time you come, turn your collar around so we'll know if you are going or coming." With that remark they were gone, but the crowd stayed on to the end.

10

Grace. What does "celibacy" mean? We hear so much about it today.

Fr. The dictionary, the first book you should have at your elbow after the Bible, says it is the same as the unmarried state.

Priests today are called celibates because if one wishes to be a priest, he must promise to remain celibate. Everyone has the natural right from God to get married if he so desires. But no one has the natural right to be ordained a priest.

St. Paul makes this clear when he says, "Let no one take to himself this honor unless he is called by God [the Church] as Aaron was [Heb. 5:4]." The priesthood, you ought to know, is supernatural. If one is called to take upon himself this honor, then he will have to exchange his natural right to marry for the supernatural honor of being a priest. When St. Paul speaks about being "called" to this state by God, he of course means the Church, God's representative on earth, in the last analysis.

If you ask me, from what I studied in history years ago on the subject, the Church under Pope Gregory Hildebrandt was the one who made the law universal that no one in the Western church might marry and still be a functioning priest. Celibacy was the law, not universally in many places before that. It took centuries for the Church to rid humanity of slavery, and it is not accomplished 100 per cent even today (witness the Moslem Arabs).

So it took the church about six centuries to prepare the members for this law which has been universal only in the Western church ever since. Today this law is being challenged through NAPC political measures. Let us pray that it will not succeed. I'm sure it wouldn't be going Her way.

If Pope Pius XI in his very first statement following his election as Pope could say "it is proximate to Faith" that the Pope must always reside at Rome, it appears that any Pope could say that the priests in the Western church must be celibate, and this also is proximate to faith. You know, people without faith make great sport of this celibacy thing. In 1950 when Pius XII defined as a dogma of faith that the Blessed Mother was "assumed into Heaven body and soul at Her Passing," one of the weekly news magazines carried a paragraph copied from a London daily. It went something like this: "What else could one expect from an old celibate? He had to find a woman some place to worship."

Let us hope such and their ilk shall discover their Blessed Mother before it is too late! One should keep in mind what Jesus said on the subject: "Not all can accept this teaching; but those to whom it has been given. For there are eunuchs who were born so from their mother's womb; and there are eunuchs who were made so by men; and there are eunuchs who have made themselves so for the sake of the kingdom of heaven. Let him accept it who can take." (Matt. 19:10-13.) (Farmers make their pigs eunuchs with a knife, and so did slaveowners do to their slaves centuries ago. When Christ was on earth, everyone knew what the word meant at that time.)

Christ is our model. So is Mary, His virgin mother. He never married; why should not priests imitate Him! Why not go Her way? Why forsake Holy Orders in order to get married and thereby take upon themselves orders that won't be altogether holy or to their liking!

The hope of those in favor of non-celibacy so as to get married is allegedly based on a shortage of priests because of so many leaving. This is nonsense. Think of the days of the oxcart when one priest covered the whole state of Indiana on horseback. It is about time there was a shortage of priests. Perhaps the priest will be truly honored then; St. Paul says, speaking the sentiments of our Lord, we must be fools for Christ's sake (Galatians). Too many priests who today would like to have their cake and eat it are saying, "For Christ's sake, don't be a fool."

This trend has been on for a long time, as I have observed. Today it is becoming a bold venture. "Pride goes before the fall" shall apply here as it did with the fallen angels, with Adam and Eve, and with all other outcasts ever since the beginning of time.

We must earn our heavenly reward. We must be dedicated. Time was when a homemaker could say to a beggar at the back door, "Here is a crust of bread for you, for Jesus' sake." Today the same beggar will be heard saying, "For Christ's sake, put a little jelly on this crust of bread." Times do change, and so do people. This is why I preach the practice of early First Communion in order that innocent children may become imitators of Jesus in their early days of innocence; that they may receive Confirmation before that. For when civilization catches up with the children, they will need both these sacraments lest present-day civilization neutralize the effects of their faith and divine love and hope by watering it down, as is going on today. Divine love must grow in their hearts, yes, in the entire person.

The laws of the Church call for the conferring and reception of each of these sacraments as soon as the use of reason arrives. We gave plenty of stories above to illustrate this.

Marge. Yes, but how about first confession?

Fr. A child that is just blossoming into the full bloom of reason surely has, as a rule, no mortal sins, not even venial sins. When that day comes, the child, seeing its parents, will surely respond to the invitation when it feels the need for confession, at least, at Easter time, if necessary.

If parents cannot rest until their newborn babe is baptized, all the greater reason why the same parents should not rest until their child has the abiding presence of Jesus in his heart. For this abiding presence, alone, as said above, was all created both as to this life and for the next. Feed the little tikes on Jesus, who is love, and they won't feel the need of physical love from others, nor will they need the sacrament of reconciliation because of misplaced physical love. I'm afraid, Marge, you failed to grasp the point made by the cardinal on First Communion. As soon as they are ripe for it, children should be admitted. Hence the first minute they are ripe, let Jesus beat Satan to their soul as guest.

We got off the subject of celibacy. Let us return to celibacy for this final word.

As indicated, it should start with early youth by the practice of purity and chastity. Many people outside the church simply do not think it possible to live a chaste life of continency outside of matrimony, whether for priests or for sisters or for anyone. As a matter of fact, it should be easier for those unmarried to remain continent and observe strict chastity outside of matrimony than for those who are married to observe conjugal chastity within marriage. It calls for preparation and willpower from pre-school age, as has been said all along. Eventually the seat of the urge atrophies. One day I was making the rounds in the hospital. An elderly man said, "Sit down. I want to ask you a question." "Go right ahead," I said. "How many concubines do you have?" he asked. "What do you want me to say?" said I. "You can't deny it, can you?" he said. "If I admit it, I have no shame," said I. "If I deny it, you will not believe me. So there is only one thing left for you to do; that would be to put a detective on my trail and have him watch me. Sir, every day I have called on you, you proceeded to inform me how smart you are with certain quotes from the Bible. Have you ever read St. Paul to the Romans 2:1?" He answered, "I've read Paul, we call him, but I don't remember what's in that particular passage. What does Paul say?" "St. Paul says, 'Judge not your neighbor, foolish man. For the things wherein you judge your neighbor you are guilty of yourself.'" "I don't understand that," he said. So I broke it down, word for word, until he said, "I guess Paul is right. I am a minister of the gospel, and I can't get along without several, so I suppose you could not do so either." I said, "You are not a minister; you are simply a no-good." Then I left.

Steve. I think it was Grace who got us off the track of

the K.K.K. with celibacy. Tell us more about your experiences.

Fr. Well, you know one day I left that last town I was speaking about and went to a new appointment as troubleshooter. It was only a day or two when an undertaker called on me. He asked me for a list of parishioners so that he might give each family a calendar for the next year. He also said he would print my name on it with etc., etc.

I said, "Oh, no, you won't. When my name goes on a calendar, then I pay for it as a matter of principle. Such would be my gift but not your gift." The gentleman persisted in getting a list of the families. I told him I had just got in town and that I as yet had no list. He kept harping away, when finally he made this remark, among others, "By the way, I never belonged to the Klu Klux Klan either." To this I replied: "Well, if you didn't, you should have." Later on I found out he was a ringleader.

Later on he sold out to a younger man from out of town. This new man recalls an interesting set of facts. One day he came to me on some official business. In the course of conversation he said, "I don't believe in nothing. There is no God. This religion stuff is all the bunk." "Sir," said I, "be careful; you're stepping on my toes. If it's the bunk, then that means I am a fraud." With that he said, "They say Jesus Christ was God. The Bible says to start His Church he picked a dozen g——d——ed saps—men who were illiterate. Now, if I were going to start a church I would pick the twelve smartest men in the world." The commandment "Thou shalt not kill" forbade me then and there to carry out my feelings. But I did reply. "That's just the point. Because you are a g——d——ed sap, you would need twelve smart men. But because Jesus is God, He gets the job done with us saps anyway. So you don't believe in religion?" "No, I don't." Then why do you have the Christmas crib and scene all lit up all night long in your front yard? That just for business?" "Yes, sir," came the reply. You see what I mean when I say it is too bad civilization neutralizes the faith of innocent children as soon as it catches up with them.

Judy. Did you prevent him from burying your people?

Fr. No, that would have been unjust, in the event someone wanted him. If they left it to my judgment, of course I steered them the other way.

You want to know something? O.K. A woman told me once that of all the remarks of our Lord the one found in Matthew 15:17-20 struck her most forcibly: "Do you not realize that whatever enters the mouth passes into the belly and is cast out into the drain? But the things that proceed out of the mouth come from the heart, and it is they that defile a man. For out of the heart come evil thoughts, murders, adulteries, immorality, thefts, false witness, blasphemies. These are the things that defile a man."

If you want to know what kind of person someone is, then listen to that person talk for a while. You'll soon learn to know what is in his heart.

Lil. Why do you preach so often about the Holy Anointing?

Fr. Because it is so very, very important. It does not mean one is going to die if one is anointed. It may mean the contrary. I would like to divest myself of some of the experiences that were associated with my priesthood the past fifty years. I would like to say a word here on the Last Anointing, or Extreme Unction, as it used to be called prior to Vatican II.

When I was in the seminary, the professor had just finished the tract on this sacrament, when I was sent to the hospital for a minor operation. During my recuperation a gentleman passing my ward happened to notice me, through the angle of the door, with a sweater on. He entered, and with apologies said, "Your sweater indicates you might be a baseball player." To that statement I said, "Yes, sir, a pitcher." He said, "Then we have much in common."

After that he was a frequent visitor. He kept me informed of his wife, who was hospitalized across and down the corridor from my ward. One day when he came, there were tears in his eyes. He said, "My wife is not expected to live." I asked him if she had been anointed. The reply was in the negative. As indicated above, the value of this sacrament was still fresh in my mind from those recent seminary lectures. So I said, "By all means go down to the office and put in a call for a priest to come and so perform." This he did. I also advised him to have the relatives on both his and her side to come and pray while the priest administered the sacrament. I had been taught that this was especially useful when the patient was too sick to pray. To quote St. James 5:15, "the prayer of faith will save the sick man, and the Lord will raise him up. . . ." In this case the wife was unconscious. Her eyes were turned completely back so you could no longer see their pupils; that's how sick she was. The priest came. Knowing that I was a seminarian, the old gentleman had me answer the ritual prayers. I observed his every move. It was my first experience. While we were waiting for the priest's coming, I instructed the relatives to kneel down and pray in the sick woman's stead when the priest came. The relatives, two or three dozen from both sides of the family, knelt down in that public hospital corridor and prayed the rosary as you never heard anyone pray. If you ever heard anyone pray, they surely did, and with such fervor, earnestness, and devotion! When the old priest had completed the ritual ceremony, that woman began to smack her lips. Her eyes came down to normal position. Consciousness returned, and she went on to get well. Days later the husband made a special visit to

the seminary to thank me for her recovery, she the mother
of thirteen girls, all because of that Holy Anointing with the
family prayers of which she was ignorant. That is going Her
way through the rosary.

I must not allow this opportunity to pass without telling
you of my own experience a year or so ago. Following a
stroke, I asked chaplain number one to anoint me. He said,
"Oh, you aren't sick enough." With that he moved along.

That same evening chaplain number two paid me a visit.
When I asked to be anointed, he said, "Oh, you aren't sick
enough." I said, "If I am not sick enough, then at least I am
old enough [73], according to Vatican II. I have a right to it.
I have not always, in life, demanded all of my rights because
it was not always the prudent thing to do. But in this case I
demand my right to be anointed." The priest finally obliged.

From the grace of that sacrament I was mentally lit up
like a Christmas tree. It gave me the light to prepare better
for death should it come. Death did not come then. It has
prepared me to enjoy ill health and to accept every discom-
fort as my purgatory here on earth where God's mercy can
be cooperated with. It impressed me more and more what life
is all about.

In the next life the mercy of God is not extended to
souls as it is here. Justice reigns supreme then. "The night
comes when no man can work," says the Bible. So demand
your rights along this line. It won't mean you are going to
die. To the contrary. If it is good for the soul then and there,
the sacrament will make the sick well.

I'm sure old sinners, myself included, need it for the welfare of their souls right then. I think that is why I got well. I've
been anointed once since. You'd be surprised how it improves
the mind, will, and heart.

During my fifty years of priestly life I made the following
observation. After anointing a person I always looked for
him either to die or to begin recovering within seventy-two

hours. Good people, unlike myself, went on to die mostly.

Out of curiosity one time I asked a Protestant doctor, a friend of mine, if he had ever noticed any difference following the reception of this sacrament. He said, "Oh, yes, but I always thought it was purely psychological." Such is rationalism pure and simple. Was it that doctor who said he never cut into a soul during surgery? He was asked, "Did you ever cut through a pain?"

Another time I asked a famous surgeon who was Jewish. He said, "Just the other day an old Catholic woman was brought in. I was called. I asked if she had been anointed. They said no. So I said, 'Anoint her, and perhaps there will be no need of an operation,' and so there wasn't," said he.

Referring to the good of the Last Holy Anointing, one time a man was semi-conscious or completely unconscious for days. Finally he got straightened out. He said to me, "You never came to see me." I said, "That's what you think. I gave you conditional absolution many times when you were semiconscious. I didn't know if you knew what was going on or not. I also anointed you." Anyway he got well.

This sacrament is destined, so say theologians, and the Church has not condemned it, to give one a straight ticket to heaven: the equivalent of martyrdom.

Judy. Why do some persons says that purgatory is a myth and a money racket?

Fr. That's because of hatred and envy and propaganda. Read my *God and Ourselves* to find out all about purgatory. Now, let me tell you a true story.

Perhaps a hundred years ago—that is not long; I've lived three-quarters of that time—well, anyway, there was a minister over in Germany. Whenever he wanted to orate with deep tones, he always talked on the subject just as you mentioned it. He had several children. The oldest boy got sick and tired of his father's preachments. The father drove the boy to go to the priest to become a Catholic. The priest, knowing the situation, said, "Wait till you are twenty-one, then come back. If you come to death's door before that, I'll come and shine you up with the last sacraments."

The boy did not come to death's door, but the wife of the preacher did. As she died the preacher said to all of the children, "Come on, kids, let us kneel down and pray for Mamma." Instinctively the preacher admitted thereby the existence as well as the value of purgatory and prayers for the dead. When the clouds of funeral and grief had more or less cleared away, that boy said to his father, "You have stormed against prayer for the dead as long as I can remember; then when Mamma died you suddenly believed in it. You prayed for her after death." The boy became a Catholic. He came to the United States and became famous when the Indians were driven out of Indiana to the reservation built for them out west. They refused to go unless Monsignor So-and-So accompanied them. The father too and the whole family came into the Church, shortly after the son did.

Lil. Many say there is no mention made in the Bible of purgatory.

Fr. The word is not mentioned there because that is a Latin word. The Bible was written either in Hebrew or in Greek. Yet the idea of purgatory is mentioned either in the Hebrew as hell or in the Greek writings as a prison, or as the place where the last farthing is paid.

11

There is a saying that coming events cast their shadows before them. Al Smith was fond of saying, "If you sow the wind, you will reap the whirlwind." We are surely reaping it today. Perhaps these remarks highly famous many, many years ago have given way to the present-day verbiage of "generation gap." The only thing new about the generation gap is the terminology.

That expression might yield to one that would incorporate all three of the foregoing expressions. Why not call it generation "yap"? The idea of generation is nothing new. There is a continuing process whereby one generation is constantly overlapping another. Generations do not begin the same day or year.

Human nature has changed but little over the many generations. Nor has the devil. It has been modified considerably by what in the newest word of the day is "ecology": the relationship of people to the environment. This embraces the news media, which have graduated from college, as have their readers. They have considerably enlarged their vocabulary.

Pat and Mike were shooting golf. Pat's tee shot landed within two feet of the cup. "Concede it," said Pat to Mike. "I'll say," responded Mike.

Today we refer to ourselves as the affluent society, and we are largely this in fact. Thirty years ago we were in a depression factually, but in desire we were an affluent society then, in the making, or at least very much so in desire.

Catholic churches were overflowing out into the streets with people making novenas to find jobs and wealth.

Today it seems a disgrace to be caught thumbing the beads of the rosary. Then it was by the grace of God for the grace and blessings of God. Today God is dead, say they. He will be brought to life again when the present affluence subsides or disappears down the drain—this, when Communism through strikes has its way, which is not Her way.

Linda. St. John in one of his epistles complains about trying to dissolve Jesus under the aegis of Satan, or the antichrist as he called him. How come?

Fr. Those who were still alive over fifty years ago could

have made the same complaint. The Volstead Act became the eighteenth amendment to the Constitution, better known as the prohibition amendment.

Just what the pure and unadulterated motivation of its promoters may have been would be difficult to prove. But one who has been trained to recognize the prints of Satan the same as he does rabbit tracks in the snow, is not long in discovering that Satan's tracks were in on the act.

Satan's tracks since kingdom come have been called and known as envy (Wisd. 2:24). The Catholic Church was getting too strong. Jesus needed to be dissolved. It all came about in this way. The Catholics fought and won World War I. Over 20 per cent of the army were Catholic; over one-third the navy were Catholic; and over one half the marines were Catholic at a time when the total Catholic population of the country was slightly less than 20 percent, if one can rely on statistics.

It is said statistics do not lie, but sometimes statisticians do. The Rainbow Division superseded even the Pilgrims who crossed over on the *Mayflower*. Such a powerful showing on the part of this minority was sufficient to engender envy, that green-eyed monster who has ever endeavored to dissolve Jesus. If Satan could dissolve Jesus by blocking the Mass, which demanded real wine, they would have it made. He would destroy the Church.

It was our friends the Jews who came to the rescue in Congress. The Jews, together with the Catholics, demanded, according to the United States Constitution, no "legislation against their religion, which called for alcoholic wine for religious purposes." So there was made by Congress an amendment to the amendment which saved the day. "For sacramental purposes" prevailed.

Tom. Did you ever have trouble in getting the children to instructions?

Fr. No, as I recall it, they came out of love. I remember a girl in about the sixth grade who came and asked me if she could be excused from religion class on the following Sunday. You know what I said? "You are such a lovely little lady I would be terribly homesick if you didn't come." You know what? The whole family of oldsters stayed at home, just for her. She never realized she was so important till I told her so. Understand, I never said no to her asking to be excused. The Bible says love is stronger than death. She came because of love. Had I said no and given her a lecture, she would have challenged me by staying away just to show that she had the freedom (false) to stay away if she so desired.

Then, the same as today in other matters, there were those Catholics of "little faith" who pulled the oars for Satan by saying, "Mass can be offered with grape juice." Much the same, they are saying now that celibacy is not of the essence of the priesthood. They erroneously said then that alcoholic content was not essential for Mass wine, whereas Jesus said it was. He prescribed *ex hoc genimine vitis,* etc., which is alcoholic wine.

George. What has happened to our Catholic news media?

Fr. Time was when Catholic newspapers were the "right arm of the bishop." They printed only truth. In time, errors of the *Menace, Yellow Jacket* and the *Fellowship Forum* succumbed to truth in Catholic papers. Eventually, with no opponents remaining of any great proportions to incite increased subscribers, the press more or less, with a few exceptions, gave way to careless prattle, such as when the fellow said to his father, "I notice that when you are telling about that fish you caught you keep changing its size for the different listeners." "That's right, son. I never tell a man more than I think he'll believe." In other words, for the past few years many have been writing their "news" in keeping with what they feel the reading public will tolerate. They have been writing mostly for money. It is already beginning to backfire in the drop-off of subscribers. That is what all this confusion is about today. The debris is being worked to the surface in the storm Pope John XXIII touched off. He wasn't so dumb. Neither is the Holy Spirit.

Well might the old bromide apply here. "My husband is an efficiency expert in a large office." "What does an efficiency expert do?" "Well, if we women did it, they'd call it nagging."

Joe. What's this new breed they are writing about?

Fr. For the young priest in my day, fifty years ago, the old-time priest had a stock-in-trade statement: "What they teach you in the seminary sounds fine in theory, but it won't work in practice." My stock reply was, as I looked ashamed at the older generation, as we are somewhat viewed today by the new breed, "The seminary theory is wonderful if you have the ingenuity to reduce it to practice." But I think today the new breed should be called the new brood. The word "brood" means the young. There were no psychologists or psychiatrists then, to speak of, although Freud had appeared on the scene with his mental lucubrations at that time. Like anything new, it tended only to exacerbate the situation. The Popes had sounded their voices throughout the world. Leo XIII had written *Rerum Novarum* shortly before I was born (1893), on a living wage or social justice and a warning on Communism. No one paid much attention to Leo XIII. It took Pius XI to come out with *Quadragesimo Anno* and inform the world that Pope Leo XIII had written much the same thing forty years before.

In recent years we have heard the expressions "social justice" and "living wage" in the halls of Congress.

Pius X, soon after his election, wrote a schedule to be followed in the election of the next Pope. Previously, what's-his-name (Rampollo) had been elected Pope, but Franz Joseph, emperor of Austria, had vetoed that election. A second hitch was taken so that Pius X, who became a saint, was elected the next Pope.

About the first thing Pius X did of great significance was to set forth in practice the fulfillment of his motto: "To restore all things in Christ." This was about 1904. To restore all things in Christ, Pius issued instructions on early and frequent Communion.

Scarce anyone paid attention to him. The old saying that laws are made to be broken seemed to rule the day. In the United States, bishop, priest and people theorized; if children made their First Communion at the age of the use of reason— seven, eight, or nine—they would not come any more to Catholic school. This is rationalism under cover: as if any great amount of teaching catechism could supersede the grace of God in Holy Communion with His love. So, today, as a punishment we are losing our Catholic schools. We sowed the wind sixty years ago; now we reap the theological whirlwind.

Imagine my stark surprise and amazement as well as indignation to learn in the seminary during the years preceding the 1920's that Pius X in 1905 had already issued a call for all to make their Communion as soon as the use of reason dawned.

In our day, at home, we were not allowed to make our First Communion until the age of twelve years complete. I happened to be almost a year younger than my classmates. That meant when they were twelve years old I had only twenty-five days still to go. Despite the fact I was the only one in the entire class who knew Deharbe's large catechism by rote from cover to cover, I had to wait until the following year, when I would be not only twelve complete but twelve years and eleven months.

In those days catechism "B's" were quite the thing. Concede it? No.

When I was ordained to the priesthood in 1921, sixteen years later, Pius X's edict on First Communion was not obeyed. Good Catholics had to wait until careless and stupid Catholics poked around to prepare themselves for it.

Believe it or not, because of certain circumstances and the vicissitudes of life I was appointed pastor to a little parish several years ahead of my time.

I had never been an assistant priest in a parish, due to ill health and the care of the orphans' villa. There was naught for me to do save to exercise that ingenuity referred to above and reduce to practice the "theory" which the old-timers insisted "would not work in practice."

Communions during the week was a thing mostly unheard of outside of the nuns. On Sunday if one wished that sacrament one had to rise and attend six-o'clock Mass—the only time the tabernacle would be opened, especially for the sisters.

It seemed to be considered some sort of sin to open the tabernacle otherwise. If a sick call came in during the day, the priest would inform the family that he would not open the tabernacle till the next day at Mass. Then he would put a host in the pyx for the sick person. It seemed the sick were to control their dying until the next day if they wished to have viaticum.

My parish happened to be en route to the hundred lakes farther north. The well-to-do would leave their homes to the south of my city, as soon as they discovered they could get Communion at my parish, at any and every Mass, even though late (10 A.M.) Mass and be well on their way to the cottage at the lake.

Gradually this got back to their parish home and because of envy, etc., etc., the law of Pius X little by little became a common practice everywhere, which it is today.

There was a law in the diocese that children had to attend the parish school, if there was a non-public school, under pain of denial of the sacraments to the child as well as to the parents.

In speaking to the bishop about the matter, I asked him if the same law should not apply to the high-schoolers. He agreed. I had already started such classes, which eventually gave way to the Catholic Youth Organizatoin.

All it takes is for someone to make the start. The rest will follow even if they do drag their feet for a while and turn the heat on you. To repeat, Harry S said it all: "If you can't take the heat, then get out of the kitchen." Is celibacy bound up in the psychosis of that remark!

If the styles change from time to time for the purpose of making money, why can't the times change also for the sake of saving souls—getting souls to love Almighty God? But let us not substitute sociology for theology in so doing.

Greg. Isn't that what the Church is for?

Fr. Precisely that is what Jesus told us. But unfortunately because it is universal the Church sometimes has too little too late. It takes time for so large a body to get in motion.

Secretary of War Baker was extolling the Church one day for what he admired. He compared the Church to the bottom of a riverbed. The bed of a river is always present to said stream of water exerting its influence, said he, as others agreed. The Church is always at the bottom of the stream of life, said he.

The comparison perhaps was apt as to saying it like it was, but that is not really what our Lord intended.

Truly the Church is to show the way, and as Vatican II pointed out, the Blessed Mother is the model or type who leads that way by Her life when on earth. It is a case of going Her way, therefore, in order to direct the stream of life. But as Pius XII said once to a black bishop in Uganda, "Why is it we always get there just too late?" It is like a President we had who was referred to as a great leader by his political friends but who in my book was rather a follower because he gave the people more what they wanted than what they needed.

When speaking about giving the people what they want, I am reminded of a certain man of the cloth. This man was in an accident on the highway. He was brought to the hospital for observation. He seemed not to be too ill. My, how he talked! To him Job of Bible fame was fiction, etc., etc.

Finally I said, "You don't preach that stuff to your people, do you?" "Oh, no, I tell them only what they want to hear." He informed me he was pastor in the largest church of the sect to which he belonged in the United States.

One day a girl (elderly) from out of town came home. She told her mother she was going to become a Catholic. Of course, that hurt her mother, who advised her to go to their own minister. The reason she came to me was to find out what to do. I said, "Obey your mother. Call on him, ask him questions about the answers you learned from the priest, then return here sometime and let me know the outcome." She returned. She said, "I was dumfounded. I discovered our own minister does not believe that Jesus is God. In fact, I could not see that he believed in much of anything."

"What does your mother think?" said I.

"She said, 'Do as you please.' You know, Mother is more of a Catholic than she realizes!"

I said, "Most Protestant people are. What got you interested?" I queried.

"I heard something on the radio about the Marian Year. I got curious and went to the priest to find out, so here I am going Her way."

If this seems to indicate that I have a complex against Protestants, please do not take it that way. This is pro God and pro truth and pro heaven, and against no one. Newman and Orestes Brownson became Catholic; they graduated to a higher level.

A short time ago I told a certain minister he was quite Catholic in his Christian ideas and that he should become a priest. I also told him many Protestants are more Catholic than they realized, that one of these days we would all be one. He said, "Yes, but not until the next generation." So if we can't make Protestants Catholic, we can make them better Protestants.

Speaking of Protestants being more Catholic than Protestant, I had this experience. When I explained the Holy Eucharist to a woman, she said, "We believe in the Real Presence of our Lord under the veil of bread." I didn't argue with her. I simply said, "The next time you see Father So-and-So, as you call your minister, ask him if your church so teaches."

The next time she returned for more lessons she said, "I asked Father So-and-So if we believe in the Real Presence. He answered, 'No, dear, that is one luxury we ministers do not claim to have.' "

She was not long in coming into the Church after that experience. She was the same person who asked if she should discontinue her friendship with her Protestant friends after "joining the Church." I said, "Of course not. Make more friends among them. Love everyone."

I told her it would be well to join a study club. I would think it over and ask some chairlady to invite her—that is, someone in keeping with her age and social stature, etc. One night she said at the study club she had heard a new one at her club. "It was stated when a woman is married by a priest she has to sleep with him the first night." "And what did you say?" "I said, 'If that is so, then I got cheated.' " I congratulated her on such a fine answer in putting to death that old fable.

Kathy. Rome has informed us that St. Christopher is really not a saint. What, then?

Fr. I can't tell you what the origin or genesis of the expression "St. Christopher" is. However, I was always under the impression that Christopher is a Latin-Greek combination for "Christ, the carrier." It seems to me it may have sprung from an old legend that went like this. A certain man from the countryside was hurrying to Mass by foot one morning. All of a sudden a swollen angry river confronted him. How would he get across, he said to himself, with the bridge already swept away! With tears in his eyes, he was accosted by a "man" who appeared out of nowhere. Ascertaining the problem, this strange man carried the tearful pedestrian across or through the stream to the other side quite safely so that he could be on his way to Mass. It was thought that the stranger was Christ the Lord.

Twice the value of St. Christopher was brought home to me personally. One time I was hurrying home so as to keep an appointment to give instruction to a "convert." I had two minutes left to go two miles in order to keep the appointment. Thoughts popped in my mind thick and forcibly, forming this sentence: "Slow down; you are going to hit something." So pronounced was this sentence in the top of my head that I argued with it to myself in these words: "What can I hit? I'm going straight down the road," as I wiggled the steering wheel. It happened that the highway (gravel in those days) and an interurban railroad ran adjacent and parallel to each other. There were huge poles that had been soaked in black pitch (yes, they do have white pitch) every so often, on which were hung the trolley line as well as the many wires carrying 32,000 volts for lighting the towns for miles around.

A car was coming toward me with bright lights. It was the time of day, about 7 P.M., when the lights on one's own car do little good. Yet without them visibility is almost nil.

A slight mist was in the air and on the windshield which the oncoming lights converted into a glare. I had been driving almost seven hours returning from a funeral that morning. My eyes were weary. At a given spot the highway and the interurban line with its posts changed places as both continued in the same direction. That meant I had to make a sharp turn to follow the gravel road. It also meant that if I didn't make that turn but drove straight ahead, I would first have to drive through the huge trolley post before continuing on down the interurban track.

Distracted or blinded by the headlights from the oncoming car, I never made the sharp turn. In failing to do so I proceeded straight ahead. Before I could think, there stood that huge pole about a foot or less in front of my radiator. I hit it at about sixty-five or seventy miles an hour (or as fast as a Buick could go in those days wide open). As the car hit the post the rear end swerved around and headed my car in the direction of the one whose bright lights had so bothered me. Well, you want to know what happened? The crash into that pole broke that pole off even with the ground and also broke it in two right above my own car. The trolley wire snapped. So did the wires carrying the 32,000 volts to light the cities. This meant that every interurban for miles around went dead; and at last counting, thirteen towns were without light, and power for the movies.

The sky was lit up for a moment like Dante's Inferno as the live wires dangled over the steel top of my car. Added to this, the new direction which the jolt gave to my own car headed me straight into the other car already mentioned.

I had to use my brakes to prevent smashing that other car at its side. From my own headlights I could see three men diving head first out of their open Ford. When they saw all the light flashing from the tangled wires, they did not take time to open the door on their car in order to escape. They just dove out head first.

No, I wasn't injured. I suppose the rubber tires insulated me from electrocution. Finally at a standstill, I got out of my car, after retrieving my black hat, and walked around to where the men were getting up off the ground, to hear one say, "Which direction did you all come from?" and another exclaimed, "—— ——, you sure were comin' some!" With that the men took off, their black faces still pale from fright.

That taught me how St. Christopher works: just like the actual grace of God in one's mind; and it will day after day if we pay attention to it, car or no car.

One day I was speeding along, when suddenly this thought spoke clearly in my mind: "Stop; you are going to have a blowout." No sooner said than done. I applied the brakes and came to a stop.

As I did so I saw a flash of fire at the right front wheel. Then I heard a powerful explosion from the same place—a flat tire. Having completely come to a stop by this time, I rationalized the contradictory procedure in this way. Since light travels faster than sound, the light was seen before the sound was heard, although the tire blew first. That let the rim run on the cement road, making the sparks, with the sound coming a split second later. Ever since then I have obeyed the mental messages of St. Christopher, no matter who he might be or where, and with gratitude. Anyway, I am still living to tell about it, after forty-five years or so.

Mary. Why did Vatican II take such a peculiar stand on the Blessed Virgin Mary? The pre-dope had it that they would tell us what she does, what she means to the Church.

Fr. Well, you said it pretty well. If I put all your words together, they spell out what the Council Fathers had in mind from the Holy Spirit. They simply told us what she is in preference to what she does in the Church. They reminded us about what Her thing is. They reminded us that she is the model for all of us to imitate and to follow in the practice of all the virtues without telling us what she does. Paul VI inserts these words: "she is the Mother of the Church."

A Catholic woman once said, "Father, you make too much of the Blessed Virgin." I am still mad about that crack. A non-Catholic once said, "You Catholics put Mary on too high a pedestal." I would forgive him for that remark because if a man is blind, he can't see. He can only guess. Without the gift of faith one needs a white cane. Let's you and I pray for those who are thus numbered among the blind and be their cane. They don't really know what they are missing.

Mary. What is the best way to explain what the grace of God is?

Fr. About the time I was ordained to the priesthood, pharmaceutical houses came out with a new sort of drug which they named vitamin. Yes, it was fifty years ago, maybe longer. Now, at the close of those fifty years the haberdashers, if that is the right word to use, have come out with an inverted version of part of that word in behalf of women's dresses. It is "miniskirt."

Everyone knows why it is called a mini or a midi or a maxi. Also, even small children have a pretty good idea of what the word vitamin stands for. Turned around, it would read "min[i]vita": a little bit of life (health). This holds in the case of sanctifying grace. For actual grace I compare it to the firefly. There is a flash every time it lifts its second set of wings as it flies along with the first set of wings. If I could recall his name, after all these years, I should give a young Presbyterian minister due credit for having been the first to present to my mind the idea that the sacraments afford the grace of God in the manner of spiritual vitamins. I still remember his idea if not his name.

As to vitamins eventually, Elkhart came out with a one-a-day brand. It may be they still do. However, only the good Lord came out with a variety for every phase of our lives—"maxivita" or vitamaxi"—one of which He called the bread of life and which we believe confers the grace of God whereby His life becomes our life and His love becomes our love. It is Jesus' one-a-day brand. "Give us this day our daily bread," He said.

This is not to say that the sacraments operate as a pill; it is to describe their effects on the soul of the recipient. The word "grace" itself describes the generosity of Jesus. It comes from the Latin word *gratis*. It is a way of saying that Jesus picks up the tab which He alone is able to pay. We get off for free. Theologians have come forward with the idea that there are two kinds: actual grace and sanctifying grace.

Actual grace operates upon the powers of the mind and will in order to enable a person to perform good acts.

Sanctifying grace is the effect on the whole soul or person which the very indwelling of the Blessed Trinity has upon that soul or person. God renders that person holy with His own presence, which is holiness. Such is the meaning of the word "sanctify."

This thought or divine revelation is to say that without sanctifying grace a person is not a whole or a complete man, according to God's blueprint. It is to utter history's mightiest paradox: if one is not divine, one is not human—one is inhuman. To speak of a rational animal is pagan, and an insult, and is to say that Jesus died in vain.

Pat. Give us one of your many experiences just to portray the power of the grace of God.

Fr. Allow me to give two experiences, please.

The first is that an unworthy person like me should ever have been put in the ranks of the priesthood by the sacrament of Holy Orders (order means "rank"), and so remained, is pretty good testimony concerning the grace of God. With

St. Paul I can say, "By the grace of God I am what I am, and His grace has not been made void in me."

Second, sit back and listen to this story. One Sunday at noon the phone rang. "This is Norma," came the voice on the other end of the long-distance line from a former parishioner of mine. "I'm desperate. I need help. You are the only person that can help me. Elmer is threatening to commit suicide. Is it possible to come see you?" "When?" "Right now." "Come ahead." The doorbell rang at exactly 2 P.M. There stood Norma with her husband, a very sick man, so he appeared. Into the house they came. Elmer plunked down on one end of the lounge. Norma sat with dignity across the room, and I took my favorite chair.

My remark "What can I do for you?" was enough to trigger Elmer off on a long, long speech divesting himself of all his mental ills. On and on Elmer talked and talked, for two hours. I listened, said nothing, save to encourage Elmer to unburden himself more and more. In the process he threw the meat ax at Norma several times. I still admire her when I think about it all. How magnificently she took it on the chin, one, two, three, time after time, without ever a word. Most would fight back; she absorbed it all. She wasn't about to defend herself as repeatedly Elmer said, "If I had the guts I'd kill myself, but I am a g—— d---- coward."

Norma was not the only one who came in for a shellacking. I, the priest, was plastered also. "My psychologist," Elmer said, "told me to stay away from that g——d——ed Catholic priest." And there he was, sitting at the priest's feet.

When I had cajoled, seemingly, the last bit of hate and life's unpleasantries from Elmer, he finally came to an end as he said, "I guess that's about all there is to say." With that I said, "Didn't you forget something?" "What?" was his quick reply. "You never asked Father what, if anything, he might have to say about your problem." You know, I learned rather early, years ago, never to offer advice unless it has first been asked for.

"Pardon me," came the retort from the well-polished gentleman. "I didn't mean to ignore you. Please have a word of your own."

"Well, you just finished saying that your psychologist advised you in no uncertain terms to stay away from the priest. I say so too. However, what you really need is to be introduced to our Lord, who is the divine psychologist. In order that this may happen you will need to take a course of instructions in His religion. This is to say you will need to identify yourself with Jesus. Note well I am not asking you to become a Catholic. I'll never do that. You will have to ask me if you might be permitted the privilege if you ever feel so inclined.

"Tomorrow, Monday, Norma will go to her nursing at the hospital as usual, and you shall return to my house at 5 P.M. prepared to be my house guest for the oncoming week. Bring along whatever clothes you care to wear by day and by night, together with the necessary changes. Bring your Protestant Bible, a notebook and a handful of pens."

With that came the usual "thank you" and the "good-bye." I decided then and there we were going Her way.

Norma and Elmer shook hands with me and started for the car. At that the thought struck me to add one important bit of advice. "Wait a minute," I called, as I went out to their car. "I want you people to promise me that you will not say a word on your way home or at home ever about what happened here today." They shook hands on it and so promised. Then I said, "Now seal your promise with a kiss." They did, and were off for home. I feared the way Elmer had abused Norma there just could be a murder on the way home with such a sick man at the wheel of the car.

Norma, when all was over after a few weeks, told me they laughed all the way home for the want of something to talk about. The crops, beautiful as they were, meant nothing to city-bred folks as topics of conversation.

Next day, sharply at 5 P.M. as per schedule, in came Elmer, suitcase and all. He was assigned to his room upstairs. Dinner was announced at 5:30. With a hearty dinner over, the two of us repaired to more comfortable chairs. Elmer with Bible and the other material at hand was all set to be introduced to the divine psychologist. To make a long story short, I gave Elmer my famous course for converts. I dropped completely all my other work, save saying daily Mass and my breviary and rosary.

I talked and talked. He listened and listened. He asked questions. He read and read pungent yet apt texts from the Bible. He took notes. This went on day after day for several days—morning, noon, and night until two in the morning sometimes.

Before going over to church for Mass, the first morning (Tuesday) I told Elmer what I was about. I extended an invitation to him to be present for Mass if he wished and told him how and where to enter the church building. He declined, with a remark that I thought was a bit distasteful. I hurried to explain there was no obligation on his part. Since he was my guest, I was merely being polite in so extending him an invitation. He was to be free as the birds to come and go—to read or to walk downtown—anything till we'd meet at breakfast in an hour.

Wednesday was a repetition of Tuesday. Talk, talk, talk. Read, read, read. Listen, listen, listen. Ask, ask, ask. Write, write, write. Study and more study. Nothing to learn by rote. Once you understand, you don't need to remember you know it. Period.

Never did I have such a good time. Thursday morning Elmer asked if he might have the pleasure of attending my Mass. "Why not?" said I. He was present. Remember, this was Thursday. Well, Thursday, shortly after lunch Elmer said,

"Say, this thing is getting under my skin. I want you to shine me up." Pretending that I had never heard him, I excused myself and went across the house into the front office to call Smitty at home and his wife to come over for 7 P.M. to be Elmer's godparents. Were they ever surprised as well as amazed! It so happened that all stores in that town were closed on Thursday P.M. That's why I called them. It was all news to them.

Smitty answered the phone. Here is the way the conversation went. "Elmer is here. I'm going to baptize him tonight at seven P.M. Will you and your wife drive over, please, and be his godparents?" "You caught me just in time. I have my hat on just ready to go over to K—— to take the afternoon off. However, nothing is so important as to help Elmer get into the Church. We'll be there." (Smitty too was a convert.)

With that settled, I returned to Elmer. "What were you saying as I took off for the other room, Elmer?" "I said, 'Shine me up. This thing is getting under my skin.' "

So the finishing touches were put to Elmer's reception, or graduation, the rest of that afternoon. At 7 P.M. he was baptized, and he made his First Communion the next morning. This was previous to Vatican II.

Norma was a practicing nurse and working. Both were in their late forties or early fifties, I suppose. Because of her work I had no way of contacting Norma. Instead, I wrote a note explaining what I had done and why. I also wrote out a copy of the baptismal record and sent both along with Elmer. Elmer proudly showed them to Norma so soon as he got home in an hour or so. Norma said, "If you ever saw a human turn statuesque, such I was, after reading your note, etc. Surprise is not the word."

Norma, also a convert, always had a hot line to the Blessed Mother with Our Lady's rosary.

On a previous page Pat asked for just one story exemplifying the operation of grace. The story of Elmer and Norma, together with the thoughts expressed by Father, show forth the influence of God's grace as a prevening factor, as a concomitant factor, as an enlightening factor, and as an accomplishing factor in every step of the course. Norma was a great devotee of the Blessed Mother and believed in going Her way.

Mankind is humpbacked from patting itself on the back for "doing what I did" "thinking what I thought," as we say, whereas every thought and motive, if good, comes from God; if evil, then from Satan. Therefore, should we never cease to pray to God to help us do His work, not our work. Such was the operation of the grace of God.

12

Elmer went home happy as could be, proud as a little child with its first Christmas toy. He became a daily communicant, and eventually he sought for and received Confirmation, on his own, at the first opportunity

Time passed swiftly, when some months later Elmer felt some unknown physical illness. He took the train to Rochester (the Mayos). Present at Mass on a Sunday, he keeled over in church after Communion time. The ushers carried him to the baby's cry room. He received the last sacraments and went to heaven. I never heard what his human psychologist said to him, but I am sure the divine psychologist said, "Come, ye blessed of my Father, possess ye the kingdom of heaven prepared for you since the foundation of the world."

Norma informed me that the human psychologist who advised Elmer to stay away from the g——d——ed priest was an ex-Catholic. I've often wondered if it was he who was testing a little three-year-old child something like this: "How many ears does a cat have? "Two," came the answer. "How many eyes does a cat have" "Two." "How many tails does a cat have?" With quick impatience the child, who was smarter than the doctor, said, "My goodness, ain't you ever seed a tat?"

You want to know something? On the Sunday Elmer died in church up at Rochester he listened to the gospel read by the Mass celebrant from Luke on the happenings at the wedding feast at Cana. During the instructions I asked him to pray to our Blessed Mother. Many times I asked him to have Her tell the divine psychologist that he, Elmer, was in need of the wine of divine love, and to change the water of his worldliness into the wine of God's otherworldliness; that he, Elmer should keep in mind that after the servants had filled the jars with water to the brim, all Jesus needed to do was to look at the water, and when He did, the water blushed and turned into wine; that he, Elmer, should be filled with tears of sorrow for his past life and Jesus would look at that sorrow and would make him blush, somewhat as He made Peter blush, after Peter's denial, merely by looking at him.

Steve. A while ago you said one should seldom give advice or counsel unless the other fellow asks for it. Just what is advice or counsel? And why did you put it the way you did?

Fr. Seeking advice or counsel or information is one of the chief parts of the virtue of prudence, whose seat is in the mind and the creation of good will.

It was stated that advice should not be proffered unless and until it is sought after, or asked for, on the basis of this rule: "A man convinced against his will is of the same opinion still."

All men are proud whether they be young or old. Pride is

an exaggerated notion of one's own mental ability. It is strongest when a child first becomes conscious of his thinking ability—at six years—then again about the age of sixteen, when the chemistry of his body has changed in preparation for manhood and giving expression to his ability. In either case, pride drives these on to learn by their own personal experience, even at the cost of learning the hard way. Unless humility is a virtue with them, as it was always with the Blessed Mother, false pride will prevail.

That is to say, the other fellow must be in the "ripe" frame of mind to receive advice or information, else he will spurn it. Our Lord said, "There are no ears so deaf as the ears that will not hear." Such are the proud.

A "ripe" mind means an open mind in a person of good will, one who identifies with Christ and His humility, who, although being God, still acted as a man when on earth. It also is one who is willing to go Her way. She was so humble!

Do you want to hear a good joke? O.K. One time a farmer sold a mule and guaranteed it in every way. The buyer demanded a demonstration. So the farmer hitched the mule to a buggy. He got hold of the lines and said, "Get up." The mule never moved. So the farmer hit him over the head with a club. The mule was then "ripe" to move. The purchaser said, "I thought you guaranteed that mule to be sound. He can't hear." The farmer replied, "Oh, he can hear, but you have to hit him over the head to get him to pay attention."

Some kids and oldsters too have to be hit over the head, learn the hard way, before they will listen or pay attention.

On the other hand, often when children seek advice or information from their parents, about all they get for an answer is a great big "No." That is to say, all they receive is a command, in place of information.

Let the following story illustrate my point. One day the phone rang. Martha was calling for an appointment. She got it. When Martha arrived, she seemed perturbed lest the priest not agree with her, so she stated. "State your problem Martha, please," said I. "Father, Joe Block wants to marry me. Shall I?" "He is not such a block if he wants you to marry him. Martha, I never tell people whom to marry. That's their business. Those who get married are the ones who will have to live together. I'll never have any part of it. What did your mother say?" "She said, 'No!' I'm afraid you will say no also."

"Never worry about that. You have come for counsel or advice, not for a command. Your dear mother gave you not one word of information. She gave you one word, no, which is a command. In order to give you advice, or information, I must know all about your case. I know your history and your family history pretty well, but about Joe Block—where is he from? Who and what is he?"

"He's from California. He used to live here when he was a young man in the fire department. What brought him here now was to bury his wife. Also, he is not a Catholic."

"How did she die?" "She died of old age mostly, it seems." "How old is Joe?" "Joe is forty-five." "How long had they been married?" "About twenty-five years." "O.K., I think I've got the picture. Now, let's analyze this thing. According to your account Joe was only twenty when he married—what's her name?" "Ida." "O.K. I suppose Ida was in her seventies when she died, anyway." "That's right."

"Well, as I get the picture Joe is a smart duck if he asked you to marry him, who is forty-five. You are a fine girl—the best. You see, Martha, I happen to know you are a wonderful girl of around twenty. That tells me that Joe would like to live the years of wedded life that he missed because he married a woman some twenty-five years his senior when he was only twenty.

"Now, lets get the full picture. I have observed, all things being normal, a couple usually have a child about nine months after they are married, maybe at ten months. Sometimes the first one comes at seven months.

"Now, let's suppose that you and Joe do get married and do have a boy in ten months or a year. You will be twenty-one then and Joe will be forty-six. Then when your boy (let's call him Joe junior) is about ten, he'll say, 'Come on, Daddy, let's go out and play baseball.' When Joe junior is ten, Daddy will be fifty-six or so. Daddy will say, 'I'm too old. I'm tired.' Junior will be hurt.

"Then, when you are old enough not to be capable of having children, say when you are forty-five or fifty, Joe senior will be sixty-five or seventy. About this time women's chief worries (sometimes) about always getting pregnant will be over. You'll be hail and hearty and will want to go to dances and socialize somewhat away from home. Your children will be old enough to be on their own, whether single or married.

"Your husband will balk at that idea; he'll say, 'I'm too old; I'm tired.' Then too, when you go to bed he'll say, 'Martha, my joints ache and I got rheumatism in my back. Won't you please rub me with liniment?' There go the gay days you were living for. Instead you can sleep with the smell of liniment all night.

"Now, Martha, that would be most wonderful if you have so much divine love and religion that you are willing to run an old people's home with one patient and little or no income except what you may earn by taking in washing or working in some factory. If such is to your free heart's content, I would say more power to you; you've got it made if you marry Joe.

"Just in case Joe should come and consult me about it, I'll tell you in advance what I'll say to him: 'Joe, you are a smart cookie. If you can get Martha to marry you, by all manner of means do take Martha on. She is a honey.'

"Martha, that is the picture as I see it. That is information. With that information, since you are a free girl you can use your freedom or liberty to do as you see fit. It matters not to me if you do or don't marry Joe.

"I am not a yes man. You earn your way to heaven in whatever manner you choose. I will earn my way to heaven in the way I have freely chosen.

"Finally, you mentioned that Joe is of a different faith than yours. That means you will always have to be in church alone. To see other wives present with their husbands at Mass worshiping together while you are present all alone will hurt plenty, so they tell me. Besides, you can go Her way alone."

So, Tom, that was advice. That was counsel. That was information which was not a command. Neither was it a confirmation of the ideas Martha had when she first came. It was a candid analysis based on truth. Do you think Martha ever married Joe? No. And was she unhappy? No.

You see, when you say no to someone, it is a sort of defiance. It crosses them up. Then they go ahead just for spite in order to prove they are free. It proves functional freedom but not moral freedom. Eve taught us the mistake in that way. She learned it from Satan, who first started the ball rolling: and Satan keeps that ball rolling all the time because of pride.

Like Eve of old they will fail to make the distinction between physical freedom and moral freedom which is not based upon a true evaluation but rather on impulse or emotion. Ask Adam and Eve and the rest of us born with the effects of original sin.

Every tub likes to sit on its own bottom, you know, and if the tub is a human being as in this case, what a price every tub is willing to pay for its pride or false freedom, either here or hereafter, or both!

How stupid can we get! Prayer to our Blessed Mother

will obviate such stupidity. She needs only to give Him a hint to make our love for Him wax warm so that the impulsive heat of Satan will have no effect on us.

Let me tell you again that the chief part of prudence or good thinking is seeking counsel from someone who knows more about the problem than you do. If prudence were hair, most of the people in the world would have to wear wigs.

Mike. Is it true, as some writers say today, that all of the Apostles were married?

Fr. Thank you for bringing up that question. Many, many of the things that are put in writing today are not written to tell the truth. They are written to excite the public; they are written to sell newspapers. Satan is always busy with his free-will concoction. It was ever thus, but perhaps not as bad, or not as pronounced, as it is today. For example, as a young man Bart Star or Johnny Unitas could have used the likes of my physique to good advantage. At the time of my coming to a new parish someone spread it on thick in the newspaper. The story stated that Father was fullback on the Notre Dame squad, where he went to school. You know, in that one sentence there were two lies. One, I never played football in all my life. My mother counseled me that *if* you were going to be a priest, it would not be fun to go through life with a busted knee or a wrenched back standing at the altar. That was counsel or information, class, that I never thought of. I still thank her for it.

Number two. The truth is, I never attended school at Notre Dame. Now you know!

All anyone knows about the Apostles for truth is that Simon, later called Peter, had a mother-in-law. The Bible says Jesus cured her of a fever. Then she got up from her sickbed and served a coffee break or something to eat, to use my imagination as many reporters do today. If Simon had a mother-in-law, then surely Simon must have had a wife at some time, and if Simon, who was always impetuous, was so with his wife, not only would his mother-in-law have had a fever, but his wife must surely have died of a fever brought on by Simon's antics.

Let's suppose for the sake of argument that all or most of them were married. Do you think all of their wives could have remained so silent that their names could entirely have escaped the gospel or epistle reporters! Now, just think a little bit. Get related to the wood "pecker" and use your head.

Jesus was a carpenter and a carpenter's son. They built boats, some tell us, from their natural imaginations. We don't know that for certain either. Anyway, Paul tells us Jesus was human. That being the case, I am sure Mary would not have reared Him as a sissy. He never acted like one when He had grown up.

Don't you suppose he went down to the lake (Galilee) many times! And don't you suppose His cousins went along for a swim or for fishing or for a boat ride! And don't you suppose that is where He first got acquainted with His brothers and sisters in religion, sometimes called "the brethren and sistern of the Lord" in the Bible! Is that where Jesus first met the men he chose for His Apostles?

If these boys grew up together, they weren't married. Besides, life expectancy then was only twenty-three years. A boy at twelve complete was the same then as our boys today at twenty-one complete.

The love that Jesus was preaching and acting and living all the time, together with His own Blessed Mother, must have been such that no gal could ever have crashed the gate with the others.

Don't let anyone feed you a myth. In speaking of myths, take the one that seems never to die. Protestants never get done speaking of the brothers and sisters of Jesus. How do they know? That problem was settled before it ever got started way back in the early days of the Church. Mary was a virgin. Sixteen centuries later there came along the Protestants, who insisted, as they still do today, that "the brethren of the Lord" mentioned in the Bible were blood brothers to Jesus. Why? The devil got his oar in here and keeps it in, in order to deny the truth of Mary and Joseph's virginity.

The next step is to deny the divinity of Christ, and at long last comes the news item today "God is dead."

Remember, when Pope John XXIII had a press conference he was kind to the reporters present? In a much nicer way than I could ever say it Pope John told them, "Your job is to report the truth, truthfully. What you wrote about me is very flattering to my pride, but there was not a bit of truth in it."

Here let me caution you about something. If people *like* you, they will blow you up (exaggerate). If they *dislike* you, they will blow you down with lies. Sometimes between the two extremes one might discover the truth—but where?

From this it is evident why we need the infallible Pope to keep us straight on the true and narrow path. Or, as Jesus said: "How narrow the gate and close the way that leads to life! And few there are who find it." (Matt. 7:14.)

"Enter by the narrow gate. For wide is the gate and broad is the way that leads to destruction, and many there are who enter that way."

That's telling it like it is. I follow John the Baptist, who quoted Scripture—Isaias, I believe it was: "Make straight the way of the Lord. The crooked shall be made straight."

Pat. What ever came of your putting all the lights out in those thirteen towns that night?

Fr. Good! I got a convert out of that fracas. Here's how it happened. A woman came to me in sympathy to see if I had been hurt. She told me she and her husband were playing cards with an out-of-town Methodist minister and his wife.

All of a sudden out went the lights. Her first impulse was to find a lamp or candle to extinguish the darkness, but her husband overruled her. Friend husband said, "They often do that when 'they' switch from one condenser or transformer to another. They'll be back on in a jiffy."

However, that jiffy never appeared. The lights did not come back on. So the wife (hostess) said, "I'll go and call the telephone operator to find out what happened." This she did. She was informed that "the Catholic priest hit a light post. The lights will be out for at least two hours."

This choice bit of news the hostess brought back to the card players, so she told me. "And what do you suppose the minister said?" "I have no idea. What did he say?" "Instantly he replied, 'I hope it broke his d—— neck.' Now, wasn't that awful for a minister to say?" said she to me.

I replied, trying to be understanding at a time when the K.K.K. was in flower, "Oh, I don't think that's so bad. I'm sure worse things have been said about priests without taking it as a personal remark. Maybe I should have."

"But what could be worse?" said she.

I retorted, "Lots of things." For a Methodist minister to be playing cards in private whereas in the pulpit he condemns Catholics for so doing, I consider to be lots worse. The first instance could have been mostly impulse, while the second could appear to be studied.

"Anyway," she went on, "that's enough for me—I want to be a Catholic. I ought to be one anyway," she said.

I said, "Everyone really should be, to the best of their ability, as Jesus both said and implied."

"I mean," she went on, "my mother was not a Catholic. She ruled the house. She did have me baptized a Catholic, but that is as far as it got. Will you take me?" "No," said I. "You have to," she said. "No, we can't take anyone into the Church unless they know what it is all about. Had you known and understood it in the first place, you would be a good Catholic today. Nobody that understands our Lord's religion and has had a taste of His love in the sacraments will remain away for long if they can remedy it."

"So you won't accept me," she continued.

"No, because free will follows truth, and you don't know the whole truth about religion as yet. I'll tell you what I will do. I'll give you a course of instructions from the Bible. Then if you are sold on it, as it is, you will ask me to receive you and then I'll have to take you in."

She is still a fine Catholic, giving testimony hither and yon to our Lord's truths, because He said, "The truth shall make you free." One must know and understand to be a true and living witness, for which purpose Jesus sent all of us, both priests and laymen and laywomen. We are to get involved and commit ourselves for Christ's sake.

13

Linda. The word "commitment" is used an awful lot today and also the word "involvement." What do they mean?

Fr. When our Lord was on earth, He said repeatedly, "I have come not to do my own will but the will of my Father who sent me." Doing the will of His Father involved doing the right thing all the time. If one is to do the right thing, this, of course gets him involved, because he must see to it that everyone within his range of influence does the right thing. This in turn comes round to the point where he commits himself and gets involved. He identifies with needy people for Christ's sake.

For example: As a priest I am committed to look after the

moral and spiritual welfare of the people in my territory—all of them, Jews or Gentiles, Catholics or Protestants. This is, to protect them. This holds also on the temporal level. Both the spiritual and corporal works of mercy are involved, as Jesus puts it.

It so happens that in the U.S.A. there is a sort of double code of morality: the one that is preached to the younger element, the other that is practiced by an older element. Previously we categorized the latter in the age bracket from thirty to sixty-five. It may better be ages from twenty to sixty-five. This class of people more than likely will refer to themselves as conservatives. Conservative is not the word; tired or apathetic is the word.

They are not out to get things done and are not about to let the youngsters go ahead and accomplish things. This is where envy comes in again. If the philosophy of their living were put into words, it would read something like this: "Don't let your religion interfere with your life. Be sure you preserve your image, and don't even miss a popularity contest. Doing the right thing is always for them to do the wrong thing."

For example, some years ago Charlie, a teenager, happened through the parish grounds at the same time I did. He said, "Father, I saw that steeplejack you have from out of town coming out of the dirty side show, out at the carnival last night." Continuing my march around the buildings, I bumped into the steeplejack, who was just coming down from atop the building. He was after more mortar for pointing up the brick chimney. I said to him, "Tell me about the side show you attended last night." He replied, "Have you got wind of that already? Father, it's the worst I ever saw. So I said, "I'm not going to harm you. Do me a favor. Tonight you and your helper go down and see if it is still operating. If so, please let me know."

In the meantime I went to the American Legion, which

had brought the carnival to town for the purpose of making money, and objected. The man said, "Father, I did not know such was going on. Leave it to me; I'll stop it. You can go and forget about it."

I replied, "No. I'll leave, but I shan't forget about it. If it's on tonight, I promise you I'll be down there personally and close it up."

About 8 P.M. the doorbell rang. There stood the steeple-jack and his helper. "It's the worst ever," they said. "Worse yet than last night." I thanked them. Putting on my coat and hat, I drove down to Frank's home. I asked him to drive me out to the circus grounds. The Roman collar I kept in my pocket as part of my detective plan. There was but one entrance to the grounds. At that entrance I remained while Franke went down to buy two tickets for us. Then we went to the other end of the grounds where the tent was located. A ticket hawker was seated on a high chair and table with stacks of silver before him ready for change.

A woman dressed as modestly as my great grandmother did in the Queen Victorian age took the tickets. We entered. The first part of the show was not illegal by civil law, but the Blessed Mother would never have put her O.K. on the variety of blondes, brunettes, and redheads on parade with their less than scant attire. Someone of them told me they were "academy" girls.

After this display the moderator said, "Now, if you'll just go into the other side of the tent, we'll give you the works for an extra fifty cents." Everyone present, all youngish men, about twenty or thirty years old, parted with an extra fifty cents.

About this time the moderator announced, "Something has happened. We can't go on with the show." "On with the show," the audience clamored. While this verbal hassle was going on, I quickly put on my Roman collar and shouted,

"Indeed something has happened! The priest is here. Make him give you your money back. Close this place up."

With this the word spread throughout the grounds, and persons who had never been in the place walked up to the high-chair ticket salesman and extended their open hands to receive ticket money. You never saw anyone so sheepish as was this fellow. As soon as a hand was cupped under his downturned face, he returned the price, and to many more than had entered. He gave out more money than he took in. Poor guy!

The next year the circus was back. So was I. As I entered the grounds someone was heard to yell, "Hey Rube!" I was informed that was the password or sign whereby all the cohorts were informed that danger was impending.

This night I kept my Roman collar on. As I walked in, the entire crowd of people turned on their heels and followed me down to the outside of the side show as I drove out the purveyor of filth. This was an example of commitment and an example of involvement. Why can't the laity do this? Where are they?

Little wonder Protestants ridicule the sacrament of confession by saying "that is where you go to get permission to commit sin." They have a point if you get their point. Theologically it is called a presumption of God's mercy.

Let us face it, every man's and every girl's body is created and formed with all the necessary parts as you have, or as our Lord and the Blessed Mother had. Also the same as your parents have.

Why be a party to such affairs! There is nothing new to learn. The animals have similar bodies. Who gets excited about animals!

Susan. At what age should a boy or girl begin steady dating?

Fr. At whatever age it would be advisable for them to marry. This, of course, must be in keeping with all the circumstances concerning or surrounding said persons in the event they should fall in love. Always look ahead to see if there are any obstacles in the way. One marries for love, not to get obstacles. Ask advice. Seek counsel from someone who knows.

Susan. What are the circumstances that play a notable part?

Fr. Ask your father and mother. They know more about your psychosomatic condition than you do. They know what kind of stuff they put into you. They also know your family background. They should be consulted as to what to look for in a future wife or husband, such as religion, education, temperament, culture, and what disparity of ages will mean in years to come. Youngsters don't know their own psychology, especially girls, so a smart woman told me once. I still remember it, and she was right.

For example: Jimmy was quite a dapper lad in the social world as a young man. He loved to sing at night clubs and cabarets. He allowed himself to fall in love with some plug of a girl who thumped the piano by ear as he sang. They married. She did not have much on the ball, but he did. He went up into high circles. He even became mayor. He had other talents. She was unable to keep up with him. He divorced her, then remarried an actress who had a lot on the ball, out of the church—for social purposes. Consult your parents for information. They know who's who.

It takes about twelve years for a couple to grow steadfast in love. Either that, or they will have been divorced long before that time. Mike and Bonnie stopped to see me one day. She said, "Do you know what day this is?" I took a long guess and said, "Your wedding anniversary." She said, "Yes." Continuing, she said, "You know, you said it would take about twelve years to iron out the wrinkles. Only last year we got it done."

Regarding your parents, always keep this in mind. They

have been married a long time and have learned a lot about married life from experience. Add to this the fact they have lived long enough to make many observations regarding the outcome of other married people, such as schoolmates or fellow townsmen.

Besides, and this is important, it just could be that your own parents are not, or were not, well mated, and are speaking from their own adverse experience. You wouldn't expect them to say so were it true, would you!

Finally, at least, sound your parents out. Get that information I wrote about previously. You don't have to do what they say, but at least you can listen.

You want to know something? I don't know how many parents use this type of weird strategy. Many have told me, "I try to break them up, but if they insist on getting married anyway, then I feel they are in love."

That's cruel. Why? Because good children have been reared to obey their parents. Thus they feel they should obey in this matter also. They don't have to obey, but politeness says children should listen. The next time they will marry regardless, but their love is still with the first one.

Always remember you can and probably will get a lemon for an automobile sometimes, and if you do, you always can trade it off for a new car. But if you get a lemon for a wife or husband, you can't trade her or him off legitimately through the divorce courts for someone else and still get to heaven. Jesus said so. Read Matthew, chapter 19.

Pray that you'll find someone in church who is praying for the same intention that you are. St. Joseph is a good patron for this. He had the best. He knows what it takes. Pray to him to find and send the right one around. Many, many persons have so performed. This may sound like being a "square," but that's what it takes.

Remember, man is the only animal that can be skinned

more than once. To land a man on the moon is technological, but to land one on earth should be theological and sociological as well as prayerful.

I recall the case of a couple that everyone remarked about, "How wonderfully are they matched!" Yet I happened to know from their own mouths that they were ill suited to each other. When in company they appeared a model couple. When they got home they hardly had the door closed when they were chewing each other out about something. They told me so.

Pat. Is it easy to get Catholics back to church?

Fr. If they are married badly, it is next to impossible unless one dies and sets the other at liberty to return. Even if there are no bad marriage problems, it is not always easy. It takes prayer. When I started out in my first years, I made a list and kept count of the calls it took. The calls I made averaged seven per couple before I got them straightened out.

Whenever I called I never brought up the matter of religion. I was adamant in my own mind they would have to be the ones to first bring up the subject of religion. That was my psychological approach. Naturally they would think it was a moneymaking scheme. I fooled them. This they would do after they had sized me up and discovered they were not going to get hurt, or that I was sincere. Lots of people, don't you know, are of that mentality.

Then, too, the devil played his part, but big. I recall one case that went like this. After the old folk had thawed out, the woman said sympathetically, "You know, after you were here the first time the woman across the street came over. She saw you come and go. She said, 'You are not going to join that Old Catholic Church, are you?' " I said, "Where does she live? In which house?"

I made a call on her so she would know how it feels to

have the neighbors butting in. That cooked her goose, and the other couple came into the Church later on with no further molestations.

Mike. I read someplace where St. Pius X appeared to someone and said, "Little do people know how powerful a priest's blessing is against the devil." What did he mean?

Fr. That's pretty plain. I don't know how to make it any clearer. When a priest gives a blessing he invokes the Blessed Trinity against Satan. I can tell you this. One night about nine the copper weatherstrip in the front door was singing in a buzz-like fashion, the only time I had ever so heard it. I went out on the front porch and found the wind was terrific. I didn't observe the sky as to whether there was a "funnel" or not. I didn't know enough, I guess, but I did make a sign of the cross towards the western dark, cloudy sky, and the wind stopped.

The next morning the newspaper carried the story: "Cyclone came straight down Highway 44 [don't look for 44 on the map] from the west for a distance of 20 miles, demolishing buildings until it got to the city [I was living in]. Then it made an abrupt turn southward around the city and continued eastward down the same highway for 60 or 70 miles until it blew itself out."

Tom. Why are some children mean and some not?

Fr. It could be because either the parents or the teachers unwittingly teach them to be so.

Tom. What is the best asset for a successful teacher to possess?

Fr. The best asset for the teacher is to be smarter than the pupil; and to show love for all of the children, especially the underprivileged.

Love is first or second. Children can scent or smell immediately if the teacher or priest has little or no love (charity) for them. Besides, never give children the idea they are getting under your skin, or they'll drive you crazy. For example, one time when I first met an assignment to a new parish, one of those ugly four-letter words was printed up higher than I could reach on the outside of the brick school. I saw it but never let on. I said nil. One day a boy came along and pointed it out to me. I said, "How long has that been there?" (I had seen it four days before that.) He said, "Four days." Then I said, "And you never wiped it off. If you were a gentleman, you would have got some other kids and a ladder and rubbed it out, out of self-respect." I didn't get tough; I merely said, "Go now and find a ladder and some help and rub it out."

That was the end of it forever afterward. If I had become wrought up about the matter and lost my cool, that same word would have been put back day after day after day, just for spite or because I had not been a gentleman.

Here's a good proof of that. A few years later I was transferred to another parish. My parting word was, "If you ever need a friend, put my name at the head of the list and buzz me."

One day quite a strip of a boy came to see me. "No," said I, "we are not allowed to marry anyone from outside our parish." Eventually bygone happenings surfaced for the sake of conversation. This young Joe was telling how he and Ronnie had been caught chewing tobacco in school when they were only in the seventh grade. He added, "There was the threat of expulsion if ever caught again. We also discussed how you would have handled the situation had you been there yet." That of course triggered my interest, so I had to inquire, "What would have happened in such an event?"

Joe said, "You would have called us up in front of the whole class and had us each take a chew of tobacco. Then you would have praised us and would have asked the rest of the class to give us a good hand. In the meantime we would have had to stand there and swallow all that tobacco juice. That would have cured us quickly. The other way we were threatened—given a challenge that if we got caught, then we'd get expelled. That never cured us."

What kid doesn't thrive on challenges and threats, etc.! So you see, class, when you get to be parents, be buddies with your children; give them lots of love and attention. Kids aren't dumb. They just act like it, as a defense mechanism.

Here's one for the books. One day little Pat, fourth-grader, said to the sister, "Can I go around to the other class-rooms and make a speech?" The sister had never heard of such a thing before. "Pat, what kind of speech do you wish to make?" "Well, you know, Sister, Father works so hard to keep the school grounds looking nice for us I just wanted to go and make a speech asking all the kids to keep off the grass and use the sidewalks." I don't know where Pat got the idea, but that is love. Pat's speech worked. He identified himself with Father and the school. He asked all to get involved. He was relating. That was religion.

A moment ago it was stated kids aren't dumb. They just act like it, as a defense mechanism. Lots of times it is far easier for them to say, "I don't know" even when they do know the answer. They don't give themselves away.

As mentioned already in this work, children should never be squelched. Their psychological reaction to squelching is like this, although they'd never be able to so express it. To be beat down once is the other fellow's fault. To be beat down a second time would be their own fault. So they prevent the second time. One time Bobby was in the first grade. He asked more questions than all the other forty kids put together. He really stole the show. I gave him an IQ test. He "broke the book," as they say. Of course, he couldn't read yet at that time. It was the Simon-Binet test. He answered questions on every grade level, including one correct answer on the twelfth-grade level. I don't know where it would have ended had he been able to read.

Bobby was just too terrific for his own welfare. Yet I dared not squelch him and ruin him for life. So I bided my time for an opportunity to slow him up a little without any offense.

One day, thought I, "Here's my chance." Frankie in the second grade asked this question: "Father, is it true that when the moon comes up, the earth shifts on its axis one sixteenth of a degree?" It so happened I had heard Lowell Thomas state as much on his radio newscast the night before. I supposed Frankie heard the same thing. So as I paced back and forth in the front of the classroom I raved and ranted by saying, "Frankie that's a lulu. That's terrific, that's a honey. Where did you get that?" All the while I was hoping to slow Bobby up. Then I said, "Bobby don't you think that is a dilly?" Bobby spoke up: "Yeah, and what's more, I think he has got you stumped too."

So never think you're outsmarting kids. You might out-talk them for their want of vocabulary or diction but not for want of brains. It will crop out in the form of contempt or hatred years and years later, as already stated. Most oldsters can seldom recall more than one or maybe two teachers who influenced their lives. They don't even remember the names of the many others. The ones they remember were the personification of love.

Marge. What's the most touching story you ever heard?

Fr. The stories about young people who do their thing on their own without having to be told. I relish the one some-one told me recently.

A young man at home was dating a girl who was away at nurse's training. Both were free at 7 P.M. It was agreed between them that he at home and she at the hospital would each be kneeling before the statue of our Blessed Mother at 7 P.M., praying for their own intentions, united together in love with the Blessed Mother and going Her way even though separated by seventy or more miles. That was faith, hope, and charity at their living best.

It is my studied opinion that each and every person born into this world shall be tried on every single virtue in the Good Book. It will be more on some virtues than on others.

Our successes and our gains will depend largely on how well we began the use of our graces at the beginning of our lives. So train your children from the start to be doers of the Word and not hearers only, thus deceiving yourselves to Jesus.

Kathy: I read in the newspaper yesterday [Palm Sunday, April 4, 1971] that in spite of physical abuse, lack of sleep and other contributing factors, the early death of Jesus of the Cross has still puzzled many who believe that He was a healthy and very active person, said so-and-so of the University of so-and-so. The article goes on to say, "The New Testament tells of a spear piercing Jesus's side, but the only Gospel that does so report it is John. He places the act of spearing after Jesus had already died."

Even Pilate, the story goes on to say, was surprised (Mark 15) that Jesus died so soon on the Cross. Acts 2:23, quotes the article, says Jesus was killed. Now they wonder if it was by the spear that Jesus was killed instead of by crucifixion.

It is also stated in the above article referred to that usually those crucified remained alive for twelve to twenty-four hours. But Jesus lived for only three hours.

Fr. You'll find it stated in Volume III of my *God and Ourselves* that they never killed Jesus. He died. That is to say, when He was ready to die, Jesus turned His human life off. They never killed Him. The quote from Acts 2:23 is not accurate if I read the Greek correctly. Looking through the eyes of sight, naturally, since Jesus died, one would be inclined to say they killed Him. But looking through the eyes of faith in reading the other reports, you'll read "with a loud voice he gave up the ghost." That is, when He was good and ready. Not until He was ready. The fact that He died in three hours rather than after twelve to twenty-four hours proves our point. Please don't be misled by today's smart boys. These matters were settled centuries ago by the Fathers of the Church, who had to contend with the same sort of thing you read in the papers. It does get people's name in the headlines today, but it is no contribution to history or science.

It is worthwhile to say the following over and over: you never heard anyone say they killed Jesus. Unwittingly everyone always says, "He died."

Even the Apostles' Creed says "crucified, died and was buried." Satisfied? Thank you.

When the record states, as mentioned above, "with a loud voice he gave up the ghost" (spirit), that statement confirms the fact that Jesus turned "it" off when He was ready. Normally, no one with all that loss of blood would be able to exclaim in a loud voice. God is and was master of His own time. He came to die, and not to be killed, says the Bible. In John 10:17-18 we read that Jesus said, "I lay down my life that I may take it up again. No one takes it from me."

In these times it seems certain persons tend to get in their own way.

Joe. Father, one time you mentioned that you hoped the pupils here would always be ladies and gentlemen so that if, as often happens, someone wrote you for a recommendation, you would be able to give us the best. Do you get many requests for recommendations?

Fr. You'd be surprised. Every year a handful comes in.

Not all at the same time, of course. They come from Uncle Sam, and all the way down to common storekeepers.

This is my policy. I never blackball anyone. If I can't endorse someone in the superlative degree, I simply throw the request in the waste basket and forget about it.

What is more, I always have the parents come and assist me in answering the questions, such as ages, dates, etc., etc. Then, after I have signed it, they take it home and make a copy for their child's scrapbook. What is important is to let the child involved read it. It is also important to let the family have it and to mail the original copy. Otherwise, you know, some people say, "He wrote a nice one, but we will never know if he mailed it." If they mail it themselves, there is no chance for mistrust.

Joe. Why would some people mistrust?

Fr. Some people judge others by themselves. You want to know something? Always be on the level with people. They will love you to death for it, especially children. If ever a child is to be discussed before the parents, insist that the child be present to hear the charges and so to defend himself. Just imagine your papa and mamma and me, three great big oldsters, talking about a little child in its absence. What chance does he have in his absence! That's no way to show love.

You want to hear a good story? O.K., then sit back and listen. Many years ago the sisters asked for a fourth classroom for the third and fourth grades. I said, "O.K., if you'll let us use that room in your living quarters which you don't use." All were agreeable. The classroom was readied to begin the new school year. I had a policy that whenever a new teacher came, she should remain out of circulation until the day school began. This would give all children a fair shake with the new teacher. Then I would introduce her to her class on opening day. This was done in order to prevent the apple polishers, who are, and whose parents are, superficial thinkers, from giving the new teacher a bum steer. Smart kids always hold back for a week or two in order to take the measurement (in their own minds) of the new teacher. Future success depends so very, very much on the first few weeks.

Well, getting back to the year of the fourth classroom, here is what happened. After Mass I accompanied the new teacher to her class in the new classroom. "Kiddies," said I, "I have come to present to you your new teacher for this year, Sister So-and-So. You know, her Reverend Mother has five thousand nuns in her community. She selected the best one of all that number which she had to send here to be your teacher.

"And, Sister, you have taught in several different schools over the years, as well as a lot of children. I'll have you know these are the finest children in the whole wide world."

At that Bobby, a little third-grader, piped up, "Father, don't spread it on too thick." Bobby realized a standard was being established by which all should live. Kids aren't dumb.

Steve. How many boys and girls have become professional people during your career?

Fr. Not nearly enough. Our children do not get enough encouragement. Yes, there is plenty of special talk on vocations but not enough success. The word vocation, as it has been used, is synonymous with the religious life.

A sister of mine, now dead, who was a nun, was the first and last one I know of to call marriage too a vocation.

I sort of liked the idea. It ties matrimony up with the sacrament. Besides, "how wonderful," said she, "if married people considered themselves called by God to help Him rear children for His kingdom of love, here and hereafter, as canon law points out!"

Steve. You haven't answered my question yet.

Fr. Let's stop and count them.

Directly speaking, over the years only two started, finished

and stayed. Too many to count started and quit for the priesthood. Too many to count were indirectly influenced. As to
sisters or nuns, several started and stayed.

George. Did you start them out of the eighth grade?

Fr. No, no, that's no good. Some came to me after the
eighth grade, but I always said, "You stay home and finish
high school. Then come and we will talk about it."

George. Why not then?

Fr. I always insisted there is no priest or no nun, no
matter how good, who can substitute for the most ordinary
Catholic parents.

I'll have you know that parents whose family name became attached to anyone that remained in the religious life
were more than ordinary. I always felt we should start talking
vocations much, much earlier than we do. But no one agrees
with me. Of course, you should detect this from much that
has already been said.

I always wanted some doctors, some professional men and
women, in any life. Such is not considered a vocation but an
avocation. I got a few. The genesis of one doctor would be
interesting.

14

Red came to me out of the eighth grade saying he wanted
to be a priest. I said, "Come back after high school." He did.
During his high-school years he was a good student and daily
communicant too, but not at my behest. I wasn't on his back
about anything, didn't need to be. He finished the philosophy
course and changed seminaries. About that time World War II
broke out. Red seemed to think Uncle Sam couldn't win
the war without him, so he joined the navy. War was in his

blood and must have formed most of his home environment. His father, a Protestant, had been in World War I. He found Red's mother in Germany, a wonderful woman, during his stretch while serving in the occupation of the Rhine. He joined the church later on, however. After doing his hitch in the navy, Red returned to the seminary. It was not long until Red wrote me somewhat as follows: "Dear Father, I have decided to discontinue my studies for the priesthood. Will it be safe for me to stop in as usual when I come home? Will you be mad at me? Red."

I wrote, as has always been my custom, immediately, some such words: "Dear Red: Why should I be mad at you if you quit? It's your life. I couldn't live it for you even if I wanted to. There is one thing that would make me mad, and that would be if you turned out to be a bum. So take up something, anything, that will be worthwhile. Something whereby you can make a contribution to the welfare of others."

The first time Red was home he stopped by to see me. He said, "I haven't the slightest idea what to do." I said, "You know, apart from the divine worship which God receives, as He asked for it in the Mass, to me the most dedicated service is that of the doctor or chiropractor. As such you would be in a position to bring physical health as well as spiritual health to your patients. How terrific it would be to say to your patient, 'I'm sorry to have to tell you, but you better say your prayers; you only have a few hours, or days, to live!' No, I don't think that would be against the oath of Hippocrates.

"You could also inform the priest in case of Catholic patients."

Red is a fine M.D. today, the best diagnostician in his state by reputation, if not in the country.

Steve. Father, you spoke of chiropractors. Lots of people don't believe in them.

Fr. That's like saying lots of people don't believe in priests or Protestant ministers. Only an ignorant bigot could say any such things. I believe in them all, with this difference. Some do more good than others. I love Billy Graham for his efforts. We have no one to match him today.

You know what? In my early days I heard an M.D. chewing out the chiropractor at a hospital banquet. Later I discovered the same M.D. was taking the train to Chicago to be treated by a chiropractor. Did you know I was dead and buried twice according to the grapevine in my first years?

The M.D.'s didn't help, but chiropractors did. What sold me to start with was a young chiropractor. He was a first cousin of mine. Such human relations afforded an opportunity to learn something about it. This was forty-eight years ago. He asked to treat the kiddies for free. So I thought a good way to test him out would be to select those kids who were already tagged with certain ailments, bring them to him and let him call the ailments. So the sister called them all down to the infirmary. It happened there were a couple kids bothered with constipation. One was a little seven-year-old (black). Every night of the world she had to take a tablespoonful of castor oil. She didn't mind. She liked it. She even licked the spoon afterwards. The very sight of it all seemed to be enough for the other kids. There were several bed wetters (enuresis) brought to the infirmary.

The doctor went up and down the spine of each one. He had never seen any child before. The sister in charge was present. She knew the ailment of each one. One by one he fingered their spines. (That's where the word chiropractor comes from: one who practices with his hands, or fingers.) As he did, the doctor was wont to say, "Sister, this one wets the bed at night." "Sister, you have to give this one [the little black] a physic every night before she goes to bed." On and on the doctor, so the sister told me, diagnosed every one accurately.

The M.D. of the institution found out about it. He raised a ruckus. I really had never known the meaning of the word bigotry until then. The M.D. was going to close the hospital, run by the same sisters if they didn't get that chiropractor out of the orphans' villa.

The performance opened my eyes, and I discovered I was a real bigot on this health thing. So are most people. Do you know what bigotry means? Look it up in your dictionary right now. You know what? My M.D. sent me to a roentgenologist for an X ray. The roentgenologist said, "You are O.K. according to the picture." The M.D. said, "You are in terrible condition. You should go west at once." Another M.D. said, "The pictures are not diagnostic." Three different statements. So I went to my cousin, the chiropractor. Here I am, since my first treatment in 1945. I could write a book on all the wonders these good people have performed. This is not to say anything against the M.D.'s. We need and can use them all. Calling people quacks who do not agree with us is not fair. Everyone has his place and his work to do. The Bible says we will have to give an account of every word, thought, and deed on judgment. Boy, it will be tough on some for the violent words against the chiropractors! I'm afraid money is involved all the way through. And the Church is so silent about it all. Yes; like the bottom of the stream, buried where it has to be silent. Too bad! Someone should speak out against all the injustices in our country. This is the year 1971. Where will it all end? What are we living for? I wonder!

You want a good story? O.K. Martha, whose name appears elsewhere in this volume, presents another interesting episode.

One day in February I was passing out the report cards. A little girl by the name of Rose came up to the desk for her card. I whispered, "How is Martha?" Back came the reply, "She is home sick," much to my surprise. When I had finished the report-card duty, I immediately went to Rose's home. Martha came to the door. She apologized for being in tears. I said, "Tell me what you are crying about and maybe I'll cry too." Martha begged off, "I'm ashamed to say it." "Don't be ashamed. You can say anything to me.' After a twisting of her arms she finally kicked through and told me what was wrong and why she was home.

It so happened that a day or so after Christmas I had performed the wedding ceremony for Martha and her fiancé, a soldier boy about her own age.

Bob, her new-found husband, was stationed down in some camp in Texas. Martha was allowed by Uncle Sam to live there with him.

One day a peculiar situation developed: a constant urge to urinate, whether needful or not. The doctor at camp bowed out of the picture and sent Martha to a specialist in St. Louis. This specialist immediately suggested surgery for micturition.

Martha wisely begged off temporarily, by saying she was all alone and knew no one in St. Louis. Instead she went to the home town of her husband to find a specialist. Here again Martha begged off, with the hope of going home to be with her mother and the local M.D.

When Martha apprised me of her condition, I asked her if she had wrenched her back. She said, "No." I said, "Oh, I don't mean necessarily of recent vintage, but perhaps quite some time ago by lifting something heavy. You know, I remember when the C.I.O. organized the second sit-down strike in the U.S.A., your dear father was caught up in that gale. I recall the day he died. He went downtown for a meeting to see if the strike would be settled that P.M. He told your mother that if the strike was settled he'd bring steak home for supper. If not he'd bring beans. He brought home beans. Then he sat down in the chair and died, right then.

"That, of course, left you, the oldest child, to do much

of what they call a man's work around the house. The thought pops in my mind that perhaps you, a teenager then, were lifting buckets or laundry tubs of water and sprained your back."

"Oh, yes," she replied. "I did sprain my back on laundry tubs, but eventually it went away." "There you are," I said. "Come on, get your coat on. We're going over to So-and-So town to the chiropractor." "But I don't believe in them," she replied. "You don't need to believe in them," I said. "This is no question of religion or faith. This is scientific. Come on along; I'll explain it all to you as we drive over." On the way this was the explaining: "I will do all the talking. The doctor will go up and down your spine. When he comes to press on the vertebra through which the nerves pass to the pelvic region, you'll jump as if he had stuck you with a knife. Then I'll say, 'Doctor, where does that nerve lead to?' and he will tell us exactly where the nerve goes.

"Now, remember, I will do all the talking. When we arrive, he'll say, 'What's wrong with the lady?' and I'll answer, 'We came to find out from you.'

"You see, it is scientifically accurate. To illustrate, Martha, take a typewriter. If you punch the letter *A* on the keyboard, the letter *A* will be printed on your paper. The same holds true here. The doctor knows out of which vertebrae every nerve passes to every part of the body."

The doctor received us. He said, "What's wrong?" I said, "I told Martha you'd tell us."

Accordingly, Martha stretched out on his table, with her face down and back up. The doctor moved his fingers along the spine, on either side. Finally as he touched a spot Martha jumped as if he had stuck a knife or pin into her back. I said, "Doctor, where does that lead to?" The doctor replied, "The nerves from this center go to the pelvic region. There are so many organs in that area no one can tell which organ may be affected." But Martha knew. The doctor gave one adjustment by pushing down on the spine gently with the palm of his hand. Instantly Martha got relief. Next day or so she returned to her young army husband. Bigots, where are you!

Duke. It sort of bothers me when tramps come to the door begging for money or food. What should one do? What do you do?

Fr. I think I know what you mean. My housekeeper told me there were ninety-five bums that came to the kitchen door last year. This didn't include those that came to the front door to beg for money. Always the housekeeper was instructed never to turn anyone away. Always give them bread and butter. If they didn't like that, then, as my mother used to say to us kids, "You are not very hungry."

One housekeeper was disobedient. She didn't obey orders. She said I went hungry during the depression. I know how it feels. So she served them bacon and eggs. It wasn't long until she had a large line of bacon-and-eggers to feed. They were local men, having slept off their drunks someplace. They came to her kitchen together for bacon and eggs in half-dozen lots of a morning.

My closest neighbor (a priest) was real sharp. He always left half of his large lawn unmowed. That kept the lazybones away. I tried it; it sure helped.

Yes, I most always gave those "driving off the bottom of the tank" at least a dollar. "This will get you down the road a ways," I would say. Later on someone would write for a baptismal certificate and with an insert of from one to five bucks; I considered this to be the biblical reward of "a hundredfold."

It worked so regularly for sure that I began to wonder if I gave for the love of God or for what money going Her way would bring in the mail or otherwise. Only once in fifty years has anyone ever paid back the money he borrowed when stopping on the highway. This boy had a new line: "My father and mother are separated. Last night my mother and I had words. I dressed in a hurry to leave home and to go down to Miami to see Grandma. I left my wallet in my other suit. Can I borrow enough money to take me to Miami?" "I have a better idea than that," said I. "There is the telephone. You call your grandmother, collect, and ask her to wire whatever money you need to the next city. There is no Western Union here. I'll loan you a few dollars to get you to the next city that has a Western Union station. Tell your grandmother how much money you are borrowing to get to that Western Union station." I listened. He did. Some weeks later when I had forgotten all about it, a letter came from Miami with the check in it for the loan I had made.

You would be surprised how many local people come around for a visit. While at my house they butter up the priest. Then in a few days the same person returns to borrow $200. The Bible says, "Neither a lender nor a borrower be." So I just give them five dollars to keep them clean with no obligation of return. They leave happy, and I'm happy too, as well as $195 ahead of the game.

The anecdotes in this volume are not listed according to chronological sequence. As different questions are raised, examples from the six different appointments have been selected as apt illustrations borrowed from the last fifty years. There seems to be something wrong with our civilization. We hear the smart boys say not to put anyone in bad faith with your chatter.

It seems to me if it takes the grace of God to put one in good faith, then it also takes the grace of God to put one in bad faith.

One of the surprises of my life came one day when the

county nurse (Protestant) visited our school, as she did all public schools and all private, or non-public, schools in the county. "I would like to ask you a question," she said. "O.K., if I can answer it." "How come your school [meaning the children] is by far the nicest in the county?" "You're just pulling my leg," said I. "Oh, no, I'm serious. I see, feel and detect a great superiority. Not a scratch on a desk." "Well, if there is a difference, I'll tell you what makes for that difference. This is a small school, so I can do what larger places perhaps can't do. I hear confessions before Mass every day. The children all go to Holy Communion every day of their own accord. They love Jesus. They live nearby the school. Mass is over by eight-thirty usually. Then the kids hurry home for a warm breakfast and back in time for nine-o'clock school. I teach religion one-half hour in two different rooms every day and three times a week in the eighth grade."

You know, I'm sold on the biblical revelation that one is not really human unless God is dwelling in one's heart and soul. In other words, you can't really educate in God's meaning of the word unless one is in the state of grace. This stuff about man being a rational animal is certainly not Christian, whether you are a Protestant or a Catholic. Who wants to be an animal!

Our Lord said when on earth, "The harvest is great, but the laborers are few. Pray ye the Lord of the harvest to send laborers into the harvest."

It has always been my conviction that the Lord is not speaking of a lack of laborers as to quantity, but as to quality. Lately I read where St. Gregory the Great said the same thing. Maybe some day we will get civilized.

When St. Paul wrote, "I am in labor until Christ be formed in you" (Gal. 4:10), he defined the purpose of sacrifice in our Lord's priesthood of which all Christians have a share (I Pet. 2:5, 9).

Rose. Father, tell us just one story or example where the power of the Blessed Mother's intercession is obvious.

Fr. Thank you. Perhaps you won't believe this account; nonetheless it is true.

We are always going Her way, you know. Here it is. It happened in World War II. It was a September morning. I had to be out of town on business; therefore I missed the regular monthly first Monday-night meeting of the Rosary Society.

When I returned, there was a telephone call. "This is Mrs. So-and-So, president of the Rosary Society. May I have an appointment?" "Yes. When?" "This afternoon if possible." "O.K., come right now." The doorbell rang. There was Mrs. President. "Father, at our regular meeting we voted to say the rosary every night in church for the duration of the war." "For what intention?" said I. "It was voted," she said, "to leave that up to the pastor." I was burned up inside but held my cool. Then I went on to say this: "That's a tall order." The reason for so saying was this. It was always my policy never to start anything I couldn't finish. Two or three such instances and your people lose confidence in you. "You know," I said, "this war can last six months or six years. Will the people persevere that long?" "Well, we voted for it," said she.

"Whatever intention we shall pray for to the Blessed Mother, I'll have to give some thought to. Next Sunday I shall so announce it from the pulpit for all to hear."

The Sunday following these remarks were made. "Your pastor has been informed that the mothers of the parish voted, in his absence, last Monday night, unanimously at their Rosary meeting, to recite the rosary for the duration of the war. They also voted that the pastor should decide for what intention.

"After several days of consideration this intention cropped up in the pastor's mind. We shall pray to the Blessed Mother for the safe return of every soldier boy in the parish to his own mother."

There were over eighty boys in War Two scattered all over the world. The war lasted not six months but six years, as everyone knows, and all the boys save one returned home safely to his mother here on earth, some after harrowing experiences.

Frankie was eighteen, a pilot in Germany. He made his fifteen missions, then was discharged. He had photographs to substantiate his story. One day the tail of his plane bomber was shot away by the enemy, but he somehow brought the plane back safely without a tail. That normally is not possible.

Charlie was on a plane during the Battle of the Bulge when the plane he was in caught fire. "Bail out," came the order from the commanding officer. Charlie, on fire, bailed out at night in enemy territory. Somehow he was able to make his way on foot to safety on our side. He got an honorable discharge. He had the hair of his head and eyebrows burned off as evidence of the truth of his story when he came home.

Albert came into my house to visit me, rattling a small metal ration box containing a bullet. Albert told this story. "We were hunting Japanese like rabbits in the grass, only this grass was higher than our heads and instead of rabbits we were looking for Japs. Suddenly the tall grass separated before me. There stood a Jap. He shot me before I could get him. His aim was directed at my heart. On that side of my uniform in my chest pocket I had this thin metal ration box with "house" matches in it to keep them dry. The shot penetrated the first side of the box, which curled up somewhat and contained the bullet that you now see. I was not hurt.

Ralph was with a crew in Alaska that went high up into the sky in order to measure the weather. (I don't know the technical terminology.) One of the motors caught fire. The captain ordered all to bail out. All did. All came down safely except Ralph.

Days afterwards Ralph was found dead on the ground. Whether he died of fright or of failure to pull the rip cord on the parachute (he was left-handed) no one will ever know.

At home we had the funeral Mass in the absence of the dead body, as it is officially called. It was a tough spot for the pastor to be in when sermon time came. The pastor took the blame for Ralph's death because he had asked all to pray that every boy would be returned home safely to his mother, little realizing that Ralph's mother's home was then in heaven. She had died when Ralph was a small boy. "Whatever He shall say to you, do you."

So our prayers were heard. Every boy eventually was returned home safely to his mother, including Ralph.

Now, will that hold you, Rose? That is what you call going Her way, which is the power of Her intercession.

It might be added here that the first, second, and third month, the church was packed for the rosary. But as time marched on the number of petitioners grew less and less until towards the end about the only members present were the sisters, aunts, and friends of Ralph.

May we pray that present-day civilization with its worldly sophistication never catches up with the rebirth of the "new man," that is, the "whole man," such as we are meant to become and to remain lest we disfigure God's image and likeness (Gen. 5:1-2) by not going Her way.

The operations of God's work *ad intra* (from within), as the theologians say, are but the eternal goings on in the family of the Blessed Trinity in love. The operations of God's work *ad extra* (outside Himself) involve the goings on since the beginnings of creation. If one has enough faith to capture this revealed idea made known throughout the Bible, let us go to His Blessed Mother by going Her way.

Steve. Quite some time ago you mentioned your success with so-called converts. What's the catch?

Fr. That is a biblical word you used. Our Lord said, "You shall catch men."

First of all, it is an insult to a person's intelligence to ask him to become a Catholic, and doubly so if he has been fed all the false propaganda that is abroad.

Second, I ask them to take a course of instructions to find out what it is all about. This will be such an eye opener it will give the lie to many things they have heard to the contrary.

Third, about the second or third lesson I ask them to pray the Lord's Our Father to God to enlighten them to see if what they are being taught is correct, and if it is not, to have the courage to reject it. In other words, to go one way or the other.

Fourth, after a few further lessons, whereby they learn about the Blessed Mother, I ask them to say the Hail Mary and to go Her way, which, of course is His way.

I recall one lovely girl. I asked her to pray the Lord's prayer the very first time she came. Periodically I checked to see if she was doing it. After several times she said, "Father, I haven't prayed since I went to D—— W——."

"You mean you quit the prayers you learned at your mother's knee?"

"Yes," came the answer. "They teach sociology down there, but no religion. They don't believe in that old-fashioned stuff."

Finally I said, "If you do not pray, then I'll quit the course of instructions. All depends on God's grace. Do your parents know that you do not pray?"

"No, they don't. They'd have a fit if they found it out, too. The head of the school is the one we saw and heard on TV. He said, 'If it's going to be Catholicism or Communism, then give us Communism.' "

"You see," said I, "if Catholicism is their hang-up, it's

got to take prayer to work the miracle of change. The sins
of the churchmen have nothing to do with our Lord and His
Blessed Mother, but rather with the devil, who gets his oars
of envy in now and then."

I have always insisted that every tub must stand on its
own bottom. That is to say, some folks like a chance to make
a choice or to exercise their liberty, right or wrong.

Besides, who is there that is not proud in mind? What
they don't know isn't knowable is the attitude of most.

It does not take long until such a one is disabused of his
own importance. Our Lord's religion with its doctrine and
many mysteries is so superb, combined with God's compelling
grace, that before one knows it, God has a pretty invigorating
hold on them.

Art. Did you always win all of those you worked on?

Fr. As I recall it, three slipped through my fingers and
did not come into the Church. In these three cases, I thought
when they started out it was a hopeless cause.

After a little practice one can sort of smell it. For example, one time a man who was a university graduate said
to me about his girlfriend, "You know what she asked me?
She said, 'Be a Catholic or I'll not marry you.' She thinks
more of God than she does of me. I couldn't marry a girl
like that," he said.

His girl was using force on him. Who wants to be forced
to do anything, much less to be forced to do the greatest
thing in the world: join the Catholic Church?

I always say, "Never, ever ask anyone to be a Catholic.
But do ask them to find out what it is all about, then make
the decision. After that you'll have to ask me if you might
have the privilege of becoming a member."

The lad mentioned above was such a pronounced secular-
ist, as well as irreligious person from birth, that when I had
him read Matthew on the subject of Mary "being found with

child" and "Joseph had in mind to put her away, privately," he thought such language had the same meaning as the present-day language of gangdom. In other words, this fellow thought St. Joseph was going to "bump her off," as he put it.

There is another important point to reconsider in the love between that girl and the boy versus her love for God and her boyfriend.

There are many kinds of love. Two are most frequently mentioned. One is love of friendship, and the other is love of benevolence. The former would be the human level; the latter would be on the supernatural, or God's, level.

Most do not think of it. But it is impossible to compare or contrast two things that are not in the same category or are on different levels.

Therefore, you just can't speak of loving your girl more than you love God. The one love is natural to you; the other love, for God, is supernatural. They are on two different levels.

15

A further point worth considering is this: How can an intelligent person prudently make a choice or decision about any matter unless or until he has sufficient knowledge? I've insisted all along that the principal part of prudence is seeking counsel or information from one who knows more about a situation than we do.

In my first parish I preached so often to my parishioners in K.K.K. days that they should tell those outside the church to investigate our religion, study it. "If you do not like it, you will not be allowed to join."

You know what? In the same town was an automobile factory (now defunct). The sales manager was a member of my parish. The first thing I knew he had parodied, if not plagiarized, my ad. "The world's greatest automobile. Look at it, ride in it, drive it. If you do not like it, you will not be asked to buy."

One year I put out a small booklet called *The Reminder.* It was done for the purpose of disabusing the K.K.K.'s of some outrageous ideas they had about marriage. Their Klud told them that Catholics considered all Protestants and non-Catholics to be bastards (illegitimate) unless they were married by the priest. These remarks were based upon a devilish idea certainly. Such would alienate anyone.

Here was the argument which they pursued. The priest is considered sacred, body and all. He must sleep with the bride the first night in order to bless the marriage and make her holy thereby, and if not, then such marriages are invalid.

The right side of this booklet carried the script. The left side was full of ads. An ad on the Catholic Church appeared. It read like this: "Learn all about the Catholic Church and its Religion. We insure the hereafter. Satisfaction guaranteed."

One day a call came for me to look at the galley sheets for approval; the printer commented on it. He was a K.K.K. He said, "You guarantee satisfaction hereafter. Suppose they don't like it; what then?" The answer came pronto, "In that case they can go to hell." That held him.

It is with pardonable pride that the following so-called convert cases are mentioned. They are so intriguing. No two are exactly alike, yet all have certain elements in common.

One day Fred and his girl came to see about a date for marriage. Of course, I pulled out the old stock-in-trade sales pitch. How about a course of instructions? She said, "I'm willing to take the instructions." Then I added, "I want you to keep in mind I'm not asking you to become a Catholic. That would not be fair or intelligent. I give you credit for being intelligent, and hope you reciprocate. You know, if you are going to live as wife with a Catholic man, you should know what makes him tick." She agreed to come a week from that day.

However, unbeknown to me her father died the next week. Naturally she never showed up for the appointment. This kept me wondering. In about three weeks they came with suitable apologies, which were readily accepted. At this point the woman dropped a bombshell.

Here's what followed: "I'm not going to take the course of instructions. My mother [stepmother] told me that right before my father died he said, 'Tell my daughter it is my wish that she does not join the Catholic Church.' I am going to respect the wish made on his deathbed," she said.

Wow! What a bombshell! Did I ever say, "Come, Holy Spirit, Ave Maria" in a hurry, And pronto the proper words were on my tongue, like this: "*If* your father said—" "Oh, I know he did. My mother would not lie. There's no if about it."

"Pardon me, since your father expressed this wish while still on this earth. I like to think he is now in heaven. If there is anything he did or said while on earth that he now regrets, I'm sure it is to have expressed that wish you mentioned. In heaven he knows what the score is and what it's all about.

"So why don't you take a course of instructions and decide for yourself whether your father, who never knew anything about the Catholic religion, now wishes he had never so expressed himself when on earth? That way you can decide what to do and also help to erase any regrets your father may still have, if any."

She became an exemplary Catholic. In a few years her

husband died. Her own family—relatives, sister, and all—figured her interest in religion would die with the death of her Catholic husband. She decided otherwise. She was sold! In fact, she brought back to the Church a careless Catholic to become her new husband. Both remain models of exemplary living even to this day.

Steve. The Blessed Mother and the Holy Spirit sure came through for you.

Fr. If you think so, listen to this. One morning at the end of Mass this bright idea crossed my mind: You better call Dr. So-and-So into your house and say this to him, "Doctor, the Holy Spirit inspired me this morning to call you in and ask you to take a course of instructions in order to help your Catholic wife to rear your lovely young children in Her way. Right now it appears the children are leaning your way. In the end the kids will become nothing. Note well, I'm not asking you to become a Catholic, but merely to understand about it so as to help your wife and children."

After a slight pause the doctor said, "Will do. When do we start?" "At your convenience; catch as catch can according to a doctor's uncertain schedule, which is most any time. I wish to add, don't tell Pat what's cooking."

This last wish, Doc was unable to keep. He did tell Pat after about the third lesson. Time passed. Our studies concluded. I so informed Doc. To this I added, "Come back in a week and let me know your decision."

Doc returned. He was silent. He said he was sold but did not know what to do. There was more silence.

Finally I asked, "May I think out loud?" "Yes," came the reply. "I suppose," I said, "the thing that is closest to you now, is your life on earth; that is, your practice of medicine is uppermost in your mind right now. Undoubtedly you wonder what this might do to your medical practice in this anti-Catholic city. May I help your thinking? Jesus said, 'What exchange shall a man make for his own soul?' He also said, 'He that thinks more of father or mother than me is not worthy of me.' Let me say this, Doctor. As to your medical practice, it will increase. When you go Her way, the Blessed Mother will see to that. There may be some knucklehead that will say, 'Now that he's a Catholic I won't have him because in the case of a pregnant woman, when it comes to a show-down, he'll have to let the mother die in order to save the child." The truth of the matter is, a good doctor will save the life of both. The word Catholic today is a dirty word. It would be better to say 'a full Christian.' "

Some years later, four of us, including the doctor, went to Ontario for fishing. We flew in a bush plane back to Lake Mystone. We were heavily loaded—the four guests, two guides, pilot, equipment, and fish. On the takeoff Doc was heard to say, "Come on, Blessed Mother, get us off the ground and we'll take it the rest of the way."

This remark served only to call to mind what everyone knows. The incidence of danger with airplanes is reserved largely to takeoff and landing. This evidently was on Doc's mind in his prayer to the Blessed Mother. He had caught onto Her way rather quickly.

Rick. You are proving your skill at being a "fisher of men."

Fr. The priest is only the instrument. As St. Paul put it, Paul plants, Apollos waters, but God gives the increase.

Here's one to prove that last statement. During the de-pression I started a baseball team in order to give the un-employed married men something to do so as to keep them out of their wives' hair. The best third baseman in town was Bob, not a Catholic. He was the most popular young man in town. His popularity derived from his family background. Yes, I pitched—incognito, under the name "Doc White"— once in a while. In those days if a priest were caught playing baseball, suspension would be the threatened verdict. I hired Bob, personally, to play on our team. The boys from the parish played for me, of course.

Today the tables are almost completely inverted—so much so—that if a priest does not play ball he may get suspended. Times do change.

Bob's popularity was born of sympathy when his mother was left with one boy and one girl as the result of his father's having been shot as a young policeman. Naturally all eyes were upon them. About this time Bob and one of my girls got thick.

I wrote a letter to Bob, unbeknown to anyone else. I told him to keep it from Laura, his fiancée. He came to the house. I said, "Bob, I'm prouder than Lucifer, and I think you are pardonably proud yourself. You know, in my own pride, if I was going to be married, I would want to be the head of the family. But as things stand now between you and Laura, there is bound to be a division. Then, when the kiddies come along, Mamma (your wife) will be whispering behind your back to them, 'Daddy is not a Catholic; he won't understand.' Now, if that were me, in my pride I would not be able to take it. I don't think you'll like it either.

"I suggest that you take a course of instructions so your wife won't be able to say that. Note, I am not asking you to become a Catholic. I'm only asking you to take a course of instructions, so you'll know what the score is, and to prevent friend wife from so whispering. After that, if you want to be a Catholic along with Laura, who is the best girl in town, then you can do as you please."

It was too much to keep from Laura. Bob told her when he began to see what it was all about. It was altogether different than he had ever heard. Yes, he asked to be received. I baptized him, etc., etc.

On Saturday P.M. I was pouring a cement floor in the

basement of the school, and who should pop in the door! Bob said, "Father, can I see you?" Immediately I took Bob over to my house. "What can I do for you?" "I want to get married right now," came the reply.

"Gee, that's kind of sudden. Any good excuse for this suddenness?" "Yes, you taught me about baptismal innocence and never to lose it. Laura and I are at that stage now."

I shook his hand for such profound faith. Then I went to the phone with a good excuse. I called the bishop for a dispensation from the three banns of matrimony for the aforesaid reason, and so received it. "When will the marriage occur?" "Tonight at eight P.M." "O.K.," said I. "Get Laura and two witnesses and any of your friends and hers, if you so desire. Come to the church and we'll have the wedding."

Thus came one ending of his life and the beginning of a new and holy life for Bob and Laura as they went Her way with frequent, almost daily Communion and the rosary.

One day Tom, the master mechanic on the railroad, told me this story.

"Father, you speak glowingly of the Blessed Mother all the time. Do you mind hearing a good story?" "Shoot," said I as I sat back to listen.

"You know, I'm retired now because of my eyesight. Many years ago my father died, leaving me to support the family. I had not yet finished the eighth grade. I got a job as messenger boy for the railroad. That meant, because the railroaders were poor, few of them had a telephone. So my job was to ride my bicycle to summon the engineers, firemen, and brakemen at all hours of the day and night as to which train they would take, and when.

"Gradually I worked my way up until I was made assistant mechanic to the master mechanic.

"One day there was a train wreck. We were short an

engine. So we were informed to have engine 101 in readiness for operation within five days. We started to rebuild said engine. The master mechanic left the job in my hands. He departed for other work. I was scared to death. So I started praying the rosary silently, as my helpers and I reconditioned that engine. I didn't know too much about it then, yet, but actually the new pieces seemed to fall right in place—no difficulty whatsoever. My boss came back to see how we were doing. Instead of five days, engine 101 was in readiness to operate within three days. I was going Her way, as you always put it." "Fine," said I. "Now I'll match that one. Up in Wisconsin, so the story runs, some farm boys with Her help or hot line (the rosary) prayed for ideas on how to cut small grain with a mechanical outfit. They got it, and that machine, crude as it was, become the forerunner of the McCormick reaper of the early twentieth century. They were going Her way too.

Judy. What was the most fantastic of all your experiences?

Fr. The first letter of your name reminds me instantly of the most fantastic story perhaps of all.

When I was in the seminary a certain professor stated that somewhere along the line in history the rabbis, in translating the Psalm "You are my son. This day I have begotten you." corrupted the text to read, "You are my friend. This day I have begotten you." Had the Hebrew word "son" been allowed to remain, it would have been proof sufficient that Jesus is the Messiah. I never forgot that statement. I had no way of proving or disproving it.

Finally, years later, when Chaplain of the hospital, I was making the rounds one day as usual. I knocked on the door. There in bed a new patient had just arrived. He was aristocratic-looking enough to have been my own father. He asked me to have a seat. One thing led to another.

Finally the gentleman exploded. I'm not over it yet. He said, "In our family as far back as anyone could trace our family tree, every family sent the firstborn son to school to become a rabbi. Of the five sons in my own family I was the eldest. Accordingly, I was sent to Moscow to learn to be a rabbi.

"One day the professor raised the question, 'Was Christ truly the Messiah sent into the world?' My teacher informed the class that if we accept the true reading of the Psalm 'You are my son. This day I have begotten thee,' we must admit that Christ was or is the Messiah. So the word 'son' was changed to read 'friend,' in order to safely deny that He was (is) the Messiah."

My newly found friend continued, "I quit school right then. I was sincere about the truth. I came to America. I became an agnostic, an atheist. I run a fruit stand." "What," I interjected, "does that make you now?" He answered, "I'm a Republican."

I think that is fantastic. I wonder how the Torah, the Jewish law, or the Pentateuch, the first five books of Moses, can be such a miserable translation without being challenged.

One day I asked a Jewish friend of mine what the Jews had to say about the Messiah. He answered, "The old-time Jews say He never came. The young Jew says He not only never came, but what is more, He is not ever going to come."

Judy. Why doesn't someone challenge this?

Fr. That is what I want to know.

Mike. That would be enough to shake a man's faith.

Fr. You want to know something? John L. Stoddard, the great lecturer, wrote a book called *Rebuilding a Lost Faith.* In this volume he tells us his experience in his own church which was along the same lines as the Jew's mentioned above: dishonesty. His trouble brought him into the Church.

Debbie. Father, you seem to be quite unshaken in

the Catholic faith. What is your best argument based on?

Fr. Our Lord's Resurrection is the first and best proof, after He had predicted it. Next, His own virgin Mother presents a terrific argument, for into Her hands God entrusted all things, and She has produced over the centuries, as history shows, up to date.

Finally, when one reads Church history about the sins and actions of the clergy, including my own, therein is a tremendous argument. Jesus promised, ". . . the gates of hell [the devil] shall not prevail against it [my Church]" (Assembly). He implied in that word "prevail" that the devil would give it a good try but would never succeed.

Jesus never promised that his Church would never be destroyed in any country. But He promised that as such it shall always be in existence. Right now the clergy are serving as the devil's tools as they did in bygone years in some places.

England was lost to the Church. So was Africa of St. Augustine's fame lost, due to the clergy. Even East Germany, at present behind the iron curtain, is being punished for its errors years ago. The Church shall always remain even if it has to go underground as it did in the days of the Catacombs.

Whenever the people with their clergy went Her way, the Church never vanished. That last sentence is no idle statement, as history shows. That statement of history cannot be gainsaid or disputed.

Then, too, look at the others who divide and subdivide because they do not have the Blessed Mother to keep them undivided and going Her way, which is His way.

Many people will not believe it, but there is every indication that the entire universe was created because of Him and Her: Jesus and the Blessed Mother.

The immensity of God, which is not understandable, has brought about in creation a situation which is highly understandable, namely, going Her way.

16

George. Tell us about your relics.

Fr. There are many success stories and many not successful. And I do not know why.

A doctor was brought to the hospital with an infected arm. He was afflicted with sugar diabetes. Apparently he had used a dirty needle on himself.

His arm was as large as my leg above the knee. I visited him repeatedly. One day I walked into his room. He was crying. He apologized for his tears.

I said, "Tell me what you are crying about and maybe I'll cry too."

"My doctor was just here and told me if my arm did not start to drain he would have to amputate in the morning."

I said, "Do you have any faith?" He said, "No, but you have." So I got my relic and put it on his arm, which had been cut with a scapel many times. His arm was dry as a bone—no seepage whatsoever.

I put the relic on his arm, then left for supper. After supper I returned. The doctor patient said, "It started draining immediately after you put that relic on." In a few days he was home and cured—no amputation.

Another time a small girl, maybe in the sixth grade, had pneumonia. She was burning up with fever. I took her temperature. It was 107, high enough to bring death. The pulse was so rapid I could not count it.

I called the nurse and so informed her. The nurse said, "You don't know how to count a pulse." She went to the room. She felt the pulse. I said, "I'm going for my relic." She said, "I'm going to call the doctor. He said if she got worse to call him."

In the meantime I laid my relic on the patient's chest. She was so hot the wax melted that held the relic in place. The doctor came, and there was no fever. He cursed for having been called out at night when there was nothing wrong.

One day a mother, green as an unripe orange, was due to have an operation the next day for gall bladder. I called to see if she minded my going out of town to a funeral of a friend the next day. She said, "No."

I asked if there was anything I could do before leaving. She said, "No." At that her husband, who had previously been cured of a heart ailment with the same relic, said, "Put your relic on her." I did, and left for out of town. The next day I hurried home expecting to find her recovering from surgery. Instead she was entirely well after having passed a gallstone "about the size of a walnut," her surgeon said, which is unique in medical circles.

One day a young boy about twelve had been run over by a two-ton truck after being knocked flat. His liver was ruptured.

I was not at home at the time. When I returned I was informed the family (Protestant) had asked for me. I knew the Protestant grandparents.

I put the relic on the boy over his liver. The next day the doctor told me he expected him to die because "when I opened him up I scooped out pieces of liver with my hand and packed it with gauze because you cannot sew the liver. I fully expect when I remove the gauze, everything else will come out." The patient was home in two weeks, a well boy.

Once a real sick woman rode on the back seat of the family car about twenty-two miles. The doctor removed most of the intestines because they were gangrenous. He said she would die during the night. I put my relic on her so she would regain consciousness in order to go to confession (she was a careless Catholic). I also used the relic upon her tummy so she would get well. Within an hour after the operation she woke up completely well.

Tom. Tell us about your "money talk."

Fr. One Sunday, in building the people up to be a little more generous, I mentioned that giving to the Lord should be considered a kind of health insurance. A man sitting in the church had his face wreathed in smiles over that remark. It sort of stunned me. So I turned the heat on. This thought came to my mind and I impulsively gave expression to it: "O.K., you think this is superstition. When one of you or your children are taken to the hospital, I'll ask the doctor for the fee you pay him."

Sure as I'm writing this, that Sunday was not over, when the man with that defiant smile telephoned and said, "Hurry, my daughter was just taken to the hospital for appendix surgery."

I beat the surgeon to the hospital. I said when he came, "Doctor, you have operated on a lot of my people. How about a check to help out in my parish?" He said, "Swell. Do you have a blank?" I said, "Yes." He said, "But your check is not on my bank." I said, "Tell me the name of your bank and I'll fix this one to suit." He said, "O.K. You fill it out and I'll sign it."

The doctor signed that check for $250.

Judy. What do you do when people are ugly?

Fr. The ugliest case, I think, I ever had involved these difficulties: praise and condemnation.

The phone rang. A woman said, "I want to see you now."

I went right then. I found the woman sick in bed. She said, "Sit down, I want to talk to you." Then she exploded with these words: "I hate you." I said, "That's fine. I hate myself, so we are in agreement." Again came the same words: "I hate you. You are the only one to whom I can make a good confession. You pull the sins right out of a person. I've gone to E— and to A— and to M— and I never make a good confession."

"What is it I do that they don't do?"

"When I confess I have bad thoughts, you follow up by asking, 'Any bad desires?' When I say, 'Yes,' then you say, 'Any actions?' and I say 'Yes.' You make me say it. The others don't. You see why I hate you? Now that I have this off my chest, I want to go to confession."

Bob. There is a lot of noise in the media these days about "identifying with the poor." Is there anything new about that?

Fr. The terminology is new and also the activities of late are new. Perhaps the country is half a century behind the times, if not more so. We used to say, "Put yourself in the other fellow's boots." It was not such classical English. But your own expression being more sophisticated, the sophisticates are becoming alerted.

Bob. What does the Bible have to say about it?

Fr. Plenty. But strange as it may seem, hardly anyone paid any attention to it until Pope John, was it, caused it to catch fire. Please read this long quote from Matthew 25:31-46:

"But when the Son of Man shall come in his majesty, and all the angels with him, then he will sit on the throne of his glory; and before him will be gathered all the nations, and he will separate them one from another, as the shepherd separates the sheep from the goats; and he will set the sheep on his right hand, but the goats on the left.

"Then the king will say to those on his right hand, 'Come, blessed of my Father, take possession of the kingdom prepared for you from the foundation of the world;

for I was hungry and you gave me to eat; I was thirsty and you gave me to drink; I was a stranger and you took me in; naked and you covered me; sick and you visited me; . . . Then the just will answer him, saying, 'Lord when did we see thee hungry, and feed thee; or thirsty, and give thee drink? And when did we see thee a stranger, and take thee in; or naked, and clothe thee? Or when did we see thee sick, or in prison, and come to thee?' And answering the king will say to them, 'Amen I say to you, as long as you did it for one of these, the least of my brethren, you did it for me.'

"Then he will say to those on his left hand, 'Depart from me, accursed ones, into the everlasting fire which was prepared for the devil and his angels. For I was hungry, and you did not give me to eat; I was thirsty and you gave me no drink; I was a stranger and you did not take me in; naked, and you did not clothe me; sick, and in prison, and you did not visit me.' Then they also will answer and say, 'Lord, when did we see thee hungry, or thirsty, or a stranger, or naked, or sick, or in prison, and did not minister to them?' Then he will answer them, saying, 'Amen I say to you, as long as you did not do it for one of these least ones, you did not do it for me.' And these will go into everlasting punishment, but the just into everlasting life."

Bob. There is no doubt about those last words getting one involved!

Fr. Yes, and while identifying with all those mentioned by our Lord, we are doing His thing while at the same time we are doing our own thing. If we know anything from the Bible we should know that God has always had a heart of compassion, which the very word mercy means.

And of His mercy, the Bible says it is above His justice.

Bob. It would appear men in the past have strayed rather far from the rules of God for the game of life, and on how to get to heaven.

Fr. You can say that again and again.

Bob. There's an old saying that has it, "If you wish to make an enemy, then you should be sure to befriend someone in need."

Fr. What you say is largely true because envy is afforded a fine opportunity to gain entrance. I would suggest you contribute to the local church's charity fund and remain anonymous, with no chance for envy to enter and at the same time for not letting your left hand know what your right hand does. Do not these words of our Lord seem to anticipate the very problem alluded to?

When St. Paul wrote, "For by grace you have been saved through faith; and that not from yourselves, for it is the gift of God; not as the outcome of works, lest anyone may boast. For his workmanship we are, created in Christ Jesus in good works," he described the name of the game of life, which is going Her way (Eph. 2:8-10).

The above texts are beautifully captured in the following poem by Father Tabb:

> My life is but a weaving
> Between my God and me,
> I may but choose the colors
> He worketh skillfully.
> Full oft He chooses sorrow
> And I in foolish pride
> Forget He sees the upper
> And I the under-side.

That is to say, at the beginning of the game of life, man's soul is akin to a piece of canvas or bare tapestry stretched across the loom of our mortal body.

Into this canvas the Creator expects the very likeness of Christ to be woven with His grace, "lest any man boast."

Under and up and through this canvas or tapestry, back and forth, day after day the silken threads furnished by one or other of the seven sacraments are to be used.

With the cooperation of one's own good intentions, the fingers of the Holy Spirit and His spouse, Mary, together with the infused virtues of faith, hope and charity plus prudence, justice, temperance, and fortitude, together with all their son and daughter virtues, become the shuttles that weave His very likeness into the canvas of the soul. At the moment of death, God the Father first removes the tapestry from the loom for the final inspection which the Church calls the particular judgment. According to the measure of Christ's likeness, then formed in us, shall our reward be. This is done by going Her way, which is His way.

If you don't think the Blessed Mother looks after Her children, then listen to these stories. I'm sure you will say to yourselves, "It is a wonder he is still alive to tell about them."

It has already been stated that my bishop sent me to a place where all of my predecessors save one, their bishop had been requested by the people to remove. Having been raised by parents who were not problem parents, which is to say they had good manners and so taught their children to have, as soon as the mail brought the new assignment, it was deemed the part of courtesy to so inform my parents before they learned of it through the public news media. I informed my parents of the nature of the parish, and asked if they had any advice. Papa answered the letter immediately. Here is what he wrote: "You ask for advice. Who am I to give a priest advice? However, I have lived a long time and have seen many priests come and go. Also have I observed the conduct of the people. Every parish has its knockers or kickers as well as its supporters. This much you will find out to be true: The good people will go to church. They will return home. They won't let out a peep. They understand the priest is not God even if at times he is a poor representative of His Master. On the other hand, you will discover that the ones who were the knockers in the past will be the very first ones to greet the new pastor. This kind of people make friends fast. They have to, because they lose their friends equally as fast. Such will be the first to knock you. Don't fall for their line." (Mama merely wrote a postscript in which she said, "Papa has said it all. There's nothing more to add. Best of luck as we pray to the Blessed Mother for your success."

Truer words were never spoken. I have so observed during the forty-six years since.

On another occasion when taking over a new assignment, I purposely remained out of circulation in order to give the kickers a break. This means to afford them no chance to polish the apple, as we say today. In order to accomplish this purpose I resorted to one of my pleasant hobbies. Years ago I discovered that certain books in the Bible, as Proverbs, Ecclesiasticus, Ecclesiastes, etc., etc., are loaded with words of wisdom of a psychological nature if one takes time to reflect on what he reads.

On the very first night of my arrival, as I was reading one of the above-mentioned biblical records, the doorbell rang.

"Good evening. Father, meet my wife. We were out taking a little ride and thought perhaps you might be a bit lonesome, so we stopped. Hope you won't mind." So went the first of their words to support the words of advice which Papa had cautioned me about on that other occasion.

With all of us seated I became a fast listener to the tons of advice given on how to run the parish, what kind of sermons to give at funerals versus weddings, how to be a good mixer, etc., etc.

After a half hour of listening, a conflict arose between

their advice and the advice just read from Proverbs as these persons rang the doorbell. That of course touched me off in a nice way. Said I, "I do want by all means to ask you for a bit of further advice. You just finished advising how to be a hail-fellow-well-met by calling real often on the people, including mostly yourselves, where I will be most welcome. You have me stumped. Please, I ask for your further advice." "What's the problem?" came the reply. "You know, when you rang the doorbell, at that precise moment was I reading these words. The book is still open at the chapter and verse, which is highly marked from previous reading, as has been my practice.

"Here is the way it reads: 'Tread not frequently over the threshold of your neighbor lest he turn on you and condemn you and despise you.'" With this reading said I to them, "You know the Holy Spirit is the primary author of the Bible. Here we are with you giving me the exact opposite advice from that which the good Lord writes. Now, what I want to know is this: Should I follow your advice or that of the Holy Spirit?"

With that, friend wife turned to her husband, and calling him by his first name, said, "——, I guess we had better be going."

From that day forward the whole family was the pastor's worst critic. It did not register with the rest of the parish because the rest of them were happy to discover someone finally that could not be wrapped around the little finger of certain apple polishers. The Blessed Mother does look after Her own if they are going Her way.

Way back when the filling stations were mostly curb service, with only a pump out in front of a garage or tool shop, it was a Sunday P.M. Father Coughlin's voice could be heard blaring from every radio that afternoon. Arriving downtown, I found a place dispensing gasoline. In order to pay I went inside where the cash register was located. The gentleman in charge said, "How about a donation for Father Coughlin's cause?" Said I, "Who is Father Coughlin?" "There you are," said the man in front of several others gathered there to kill time. "You know, I have collected several dollars from the Masons for this cause and here comes one priest and doesn't even know who he is."

Here it is useful to call attention to the fact that in life's struggle and conflicts there is such a thing as feinting, as it is called in boxing. The man in question, an unbeliever and an atheist with his mother's milk, was sounding off. After his Masonic bragging I let him have it: "Yes," said I, "since Father Coughlin is telling you how to save your money, you are hanging on his lips. If he told you how to save your souls for heaven, you'd turn off the radio."

Joe. Was there ever any aftermath to that episode?

Fr. You've got the faith, Joe. You seem to sense that Our Lady takes care of Her own.

Indeed there was a great aftermath. One day many years later the phone rang; and who do you suppose was calling? The very atheist who had chewed me out before others was telephoning from his own home as an invalid to come to his house and baptize him.

I knew his sisters were Catholic haters. Both were present in the room, entered by the front door. As I knocked and entered in response to a "Come in" there were his two sisters. At once the man said, "I want to be baptized." I wasn't sure the sisters had heard him ask for it, so I said, "You'll have to speak louder." With his booming voice he repeated his request, "I want to be baptized." Never after could they say, as is the practice of saying, that while they are unconscious the priest comes and steals them. How little do they know whereof they speak! One must desire Baptism freely, knowingly, and willingly. If God does not force anyone to become a child of His, how can anyone else!

Pat. What was that episode about the free clinic, since we are reminiscing?

Fr. During the depression the Lions Club invited the priest to a special meeting. This meeting was set up to discuss ways and means of building a free clinic on wheels downtown. Poor people were to have their tonsils removed for free, as well as dental work. As usual the club was to sponsor it, but the rank and file of the people were to furnish the money for doctors' fees, etc., etc.

After several of the big wheels had had their say, finally the priest was called upon—last, thank goodness. This happened about the time Pius XI's *Quadragesimo Anno* encyclical came out on social justice and living wage. Perhaps the audience had never read it, or even maybe never heard of it, but the priest had. In a nutshell the priest said, "If all of us paid an honest living wage the people would be able to pay their own doctor bills, and there would be no embarrassment coming from being on welfare or charity." Wages went up and the Lions went down and there never was heard another word about a free clinic. People by and large are honest if given a chance. They recognize the sincerity in one even if it is not always said with flowers. God's grace sees to that, and the Blessed Mother is the dispenser of that grace for those who are going Her way.

Mike. How about the time our fair town was put on the map all over the world, together with its pastor, by the judge of the circuit court?

Fr. I'm afraid you did not properly state the case. It was not the judge but rather his political enemies that used the press to smear him, while the pastor sought to spare him the injustice.

Here is the way the case happened. One of my boys (8th grade) and two boys past the age of twenty-one went through a skylight into a grocery store and stole some candy, cigarettes, etc. They were caught. The older boys received a mandatory sentence. My boy, being only fourteen, was subject to clemency on the part of the judge.

Knowing this, I appeared before the judge asking for clemency and to have the boy paroled to me. The judge said, "Wait till the boy appears in court. Only then will I make up my mind. You know, Father, most of the time when these boys appear in court they walk in with a defiant swagger, and most always with the collar to their shirt unbuttoned, as if they owned the world. There is not the slightest sign of remorse."

When my boy entered the courtroom, his comportment ran true to the judge's description. Seeing this, the judge decided to soften the boy up a little. The judge called for the chief of police, who had made the original arrest. The judge instructed the chief to ascertain what the weight of the stolen property may have been, and then to have the boy carry anything that would be the equivalent in weight. With that the judge took off for Chicago to see the Cubs or the Sox over the weekend. I failed to add that the boy was to carry this small weight to and fro from the county seat to the boy's home town, which was my parish.

Through some misunderstanding the police chief had the boy carry a sack of bricks weighing over twenty-five pounds to and fro, with the added instruction that the boy stop at Mass on Sunday morning in his home town.

It was no sooner ordered than the orders of the judge were blown up—I mean, enlarged upon by his political enemies. The press made such a great story out of it that three newsreel people, one of which was Pathé, sent news trucks with equipment for recording and photographing down to our fair town. By this time the boy was fast becoming a hero, an international hero with blistered feet from walking, as the press lambasted the judge.

The judge being gone out of town, I took it upon myself to countermand the order of walking to and fro. The walking business was not in reality a sentence (official) by the judge but merely an imposed punishment to bring the boy to his senses so the judge in good heart and graces might dismiss the case.

The thing that incensed me about it all was the fact that the three news trucks that drove down from Chicago drove over the two lovely clay tennis courts which I personally had constructed at much labor; and this soon after a rain when their tracks cut in deeply.

One of the ushers in the church that morning (Sunday) at the eight-o'clock Mass used his head and came dashing into the sacristy to tell me the newsboys wanted the culprit and his pastor to appear on the front steps of the church for speeches and pictures. I told the usher to hurry and bring my boy to the sacristy at once. By that time one of the news boys was sort of taking over possession of things as if he owned the place.

Guess what! He was talking all over the place in church, a thing we never do. On top of that he was chewing out the judge, my friend, who had paroled several of my boys to me and who I hoped would also parole this lad to me. On top of all this, mind you, he had a speech for the boy and also a speech for the priest to read from the church steps against the judge for his sound-picture machine.

Still smarting about my ruined tennis courts and the injustices to the judge, I gave a speech which they wished afterwards they had recorded.

You know what one of them said? "I'm the guy that shot the St. Bartholomew's Day massacre in Chicago, and I come down to this little jerk-water town and get shot instead."

Going Her way pays big dividends if you stay hitched with faith.

Joe. Wasn't this same boy implicated in the storming of a man's house one night?

Fr. You have a good memory. That is correct. You know, one night I decided to go to bed early. I was no sooner in bed when the phone rang. It was the city clerk calling. She said, "They are storming Joe's house, and the police won't do a thing. Only you can stop it." I'm not a policeman, thought I. However, I never did say no to anyone where there was a case of involvement. Accordingly I got up, dressed and drove downtown, where Joe's fashionable residence was located. In fact, it blocked the street which detours around it. I parked a block away, got out of my car and listened to the window glass rattle as stones were bandied about. I could see the police in uniform but most inactive. A bunch of boys were in the yard doing dirty work. The oldsters in large number graced the sidewalks as the performance continued with no reaction from the police whatever. A few seconds of this and the injustice of it all propelled me up into the yard of Joe's home. I attempted to address the teenagers. As I did they booed me. My reaction was for more, more, more, more boos. "I love it; it makes me homesick. I was raised on a ranch full of cattle. Your boos make me homesick. I love it." You know what? They never let out another boo after that, nor did anyone throw a stone or tomato at me. Then I addressed myself to the oldsters who lined the sidewalks all around the building but out of danger. "You oldsters, go home. This is all your fault because you are aiding and abetting this thing by your very presence. These youngsters are merely showing off for your benefit manifested by the very approval because of your presence here tonight." The oldsters went home and the kids disappeared. It was easy.

Now let me climax these stories with one that you will consider a lulu.

One evening after supper the phone rang. A woman's

voice said, "I am from ———. Might I see you?" "Yes," said I. "When?" "Right now."

In a few minutes the door bell rang. There stood a young woman. Politely I received her and asked what I might do for her. That was enough to set her off on a verbal barrage about her husband and his drinking, and how I should talk to him. It developed that he was waiting outside in their automobile. After an hour's worth of instructions from her, she went outside and brought him in. This touched off another barrage of talk about, and against, her husband who always came home drunk at five o'clock working time.

All the while I was studying the nice looking man. It had developed that the man had recently returned from war and that while in the service he had taken advantage of the GI Bill for soldiers to attend a university. In this case it was Indiana U.

I asked him what was his best subject. He said, "Mathematics."

That gave me an idea as to his mentality, as well as to his character when pinned against a wife who was so volatile.

I excused myself and went out to the kitchen. There I found a large medicine bottle. So I soaked the label with hot water for its removal. Then I filled said bottle with water from the tap and took it to the woman. I said, "This is miracle water. When you see your husband coming down the street be sure to take a mouthful of this miracle. Neither spit it out nor swallow that mouthful of water for an hour after your husband comes home. This will kill your husband's urge to get drunk." My mind told me that he drank in order to face the "music" from his wife. It cured both of them. Such was the effect of the miracle water.

Later on, she returned to find out what it would take to become a mother. I said, "Go to chiropractor ——— and have him loosen you up. That worked too. She wrote me a very gratifying letter on both counts later on. I also asked them to go Her way in their prayers, which they did. On and on one might go but these are some of the stories that come quickly to my mind.

Tom. But how do you remember all these things as if it were yesterday, when in reality it has been thirty or forty years or more?

Fr. I told you many times I once made a deal with the Blessed Mother and the Holy Spirit if they would tell me what to do and what to say, I would do it and would say it and also take the heat. Do you remember our Lord's words to His Apostles where He said about that memory thing, "When he the Holy Spirit comes he will recall all things to your mind whatsoever I will have said to you? And what you shall say"? Our Blessed Mother will never let us down, because She and the Holy Spirit are as one, even more so than your own father and mother.

You want to know a funny one? In the early days of the thirties when the second sit-down strike in the country after Bendix in South Bend was pulled off in our town, some of my people were involved. However, on a Sunday the women of my parish who worked there crawled out a window to come to Mass, and of course to hear what the pastor might have to say. At sermon time I said nothing because I was afraid it would distract them that they might not be able to participate properly in the Mass. When Mass was over, however, I turned and said, "Any of you men who have a wife or a daughter in on that sit-down strike, please inform them they are violating the Seventh Commandment, and they had better leave."

Mostly women worked there only. When my women returned to the plant after Mass, the Protestants and others rushed to ask, "What did Father have to say?" "He said those sit-downers are violating the Seventh Commandment." Finally some Protestant came up with what the reading of the Seventh Commandment is. "Oh, yes," she said. 'Thou shalt not commit adultery.' " "Well, he's right because we have four divorces pending now for that very reason, all of which occurred during this strike."

The joke of the matter is that the Catholic reading of the Seventh Commandment to which I had referred has to do with injustice. This is not to say that all strikes are unjust. But that one surely was.